MY NAME
MEANS FIRE

MY NAME MEANS FIRE

a memoir

ATASH YAGHMAIAN

BEACON PRESS, BOSTON

Beacon Press
24 Farnsworth Street
Boston, Massachusetts
www.beacon.org

Beacon Press books
are published under the auspices of
the Unitarian Universalist Association of Congregations.

28 27 26 25   8 7 6 5 4 3 2 1

This book is printed on acid-free paper that meets the uncoated paper
ANSI/NISO specifications for permanence as revised in 1992.

Text design and composition by Kim Arney

*Library of Congress Cataloging-in-Publication
Data is available for this title.*
ISBN: 978-0-8070-2072-2; e-book: 978-0-8070-2073-9;
audiobook: 978-0-8070-2224-5

The authorized representative in the EU for product safety and
compliance is Easy Access System Europe 16879218, Mustamäe tee 50,
10621 Tallinn, Estonia: http://beacon.org/eu-contact.

To Atashee (Red), my youngest part, for her resilience, patience, and creativity, which kept me alive and made me the woman I am. Without you, none of this would be possible.

CONTENTS

LETTER TO THE READER

Dear Reader,

Wherever I go, whenever I share pieces of my story and the brutal things that happened to me as a child, I always get asked the same question: "But how did you survive?"

The truth is that, for many decades, I didn't have an answer. That is, until I began writing this memoir.

I used to think I survived because I was lucky. But how lucky was I, exactly, if all these bad things still happened? I knew I was odd, because everyone told me so since I could remember. As a kid, they called me "The Girl Who Stares at Walls."

As a child, my home life was unpredictable: a confusing mix of love and terror. I was neglected and discarded by my caretakers and easily targeted by pedophiles. I was sexually abused for the first time at the age of five, and this abuse continued, from both strangers and relatives, until I escaped Iran in my late teens.

Outside my home, Iran was also on fire. During the eight-year war with Iraq that followed the revolution, I went to sleep many nights to the sound of bombs falling on Tehran. Daily sirens interrupted our meals, our school lessons, and our card games, and ushered us into basements where each family had built a bomb shelter. No electric lights, for fear Iraqi planes might see our homes.

I didn't feel safe inside my home or outside of it. So I left reality. Just like that. I dissociated into a place I called the House of Stone: a building in a magical forest full of peaceful creatures, and kind, talking trees, and even volcanoes that spit fire at anyone who wanted to hurt me. This place was my salvation.

I didn't know that, as this was going on, I was also losing touch with reality. I didn't want to live in a reality of abuse, war, violence, and despair. My family's solution to my problems was to try to marry me off to anyone who could pay a good price for me. I understood that, to be truly free, I had to leave my family, the House, and Iran for good.

I thought things would be different when I grew up and later left Iran, but this mystery of losing touch with reality just traveled with me. Eventually, I found a therapist who diagnosed me with dissociative identity disorder (DID). This wasn't the first time I'd heard the term, but I'd always thought of multiple personalities as something only evil people had. But I could no longer deny the truth of my multiplicity. I embraced it and found an answer to the question "But how did you survive?"

For years before accepting who I am, I managed my dissociation by keeping myself busy with work and studies. I left romantic relationships as soon as partners started noticing that a different part of me was more present on different days. Gradually, I began to understand that my House of Stone wasn't just a fantasy. The "people" in it were different parts of me, different personalities, each represented by a unique color. In the House, they could all interact, but in my life outside this place, they were separated from one another by amnesia, unable to share each other's memories or experiences.

After years of hiding, I have come to understand that my condition—DID—is exactly what has saved my life. As a child, if I had experienced how devastating my life was, I wouldn't have survived. Far from being a curse, DID has been a gift, a coping mechanism that allowed me to survive.

As a therapist, I have become dismayed with the stigma attached to disassociation in the field of psychology, to say nothing of the stigma attached to it in the media. I've heard many colleagues say that people like me are "too crazy" or "too hopeless" to treat rather than seeing dissociation as the lifesaver it can be and has been for me. For many years, I felt like a freak, but through the many trauma survivors I've worked with, I've come to see the blessing in dissociation and am determined to tell my story now in order to give hope to others. The truth is everyone dissociates to some extent, even if they don't have DID, and everyone carries shame around with them while mourning their own loss of focus and memory. This shame, I have found, is a barrier to healing. My book is therefore part of a collective healing process.

The process of writing itself has been integral in remembering, healing, and integrating different parts of myself that had been fragmented and exiled through trauma. I wrote this book by allowing each of my parts to tell their story and then stitching these together into one brocade. To do that, I have preserved a single narrative in the narration of my outer life, but I have allowed my different parts to tell the separate stories of my inner world. The process of writing down my multiplicity transparently was a stark contrast to how I had lived for many years.

Today, I know that my name—Atash, meaning fire—can be a source of healing, not a source of harm. Fire warms, transforms, and lights the way. I know my story will bring hope and a path to those currently lost in their darkness.

1

MY NAME MEANS FIRE

My father met my mother while she was working as the head supervisor at Revlon, at the Kooroosh Mall in Tehran. My father was a salesman who found himself in the position of having to answer to my mother. He was dumbstruck whenever he had to sit in a meeting with her. I once saw a picture of a time when the shah himself came to visit her cosmetics department. In it, the king is wearing a sharp black suit and kissing my mother's hand; he has a mesmerized look on his face. My father stands in the background, a scrawny young man in an ill-fitting suit. My mother's beauty was legendary: in the picture her twenty-two-year-old body was lean and strong; her big hazel eyes were magnificent and confident. My father was determined, and nothing could stop him from trying to win her. He sent his own mother to ask for her hand in marriage. She said no, without hesitation. She knew she could do better.

That same night, my mother got a call from the hospital: my father had tried to kill himself, the nurse told her. Hearing the news, my mother ran over and begged my father's forgiveness for having laughed at his love-confession. What might have been a red flag for some was exactly the sign she was waiting for: a man who would give his life for her. She married him as soon as soon as he was released from the hospital.

After she agreed to marry him, they never left each other's sight. Pretty soon, my mother was pregnant with a boy. My brother gave her immense pride, since she believed that a son is what keeps a couple together. They got it "right" the first time; now everything else was a bonus. Or should have been.

A year later, my mother was pregnant with a girl: me. A change came over her. Whereas before she had been content to come home after work to cook and clean for my father, now, with me in her belly, she felt a desire to go out every night. All she wanted to do was dance. She'd dance on tables at parties, dance anywhere and everywhere she could. She seemed to have unlimited energy. My father watched this change with curiosity. People used to come up to him and say, "There's a fire in your wife's belly," and so my father called me "Atash," which means fire in Persian.

Why my father left our family was a mystery to me for many years. My uncles and grandmother said it was because of my mother's jealousy. They used to tell me stories about how she would interrogate him whenever he left the house, asking where he was going and who he was seeing. My father's own mother, Maman Moneer, says there was a time when she had to come to our street and meet my father behind a tree, because my mother was jealous even of his relationship with her. Anytime he'd go out, she was sure he was meeting another woman.

My father would try to console my mother, saying, "Don't you know how beautiful you are? Why would I ever look elsewhere?" "Your mother was crazy back then," my uncles used to say to me. "There was nothing else for your father to do but leave."

My mother has a different theory, however. She became convinced that by agreeing to name me Atash, she had unknowingly inflicted a curse on her marriage. "Why did I let your father name you that?" she'd say. "Fire has a spirit, as do all of the elements. With that name, you brought a spirit into my life, one that burned my marriage."

I would cry when my mother talked like that to me and I'd run up to bed. Sometimes, she'd try to comfort me after. "It's not you who are bad," she'd say. "It's just your name." But Atash was my name, and I couldn't separate from it. Even as a young child, I felt responsible for breaking up my parents' marriage. I wished I could disappear and not be the burden that destroyed their perfect love. I was also worried that the fire-spirit might hurt me too.

Divorce is a taboo in Iran, and couples tend to stay together even if they are unhappy. My parents divorced before I turned one year old, which meant that my mother was now isolated from everyone except her own mother, Maman Bozorg. So my mother, brother, and I were forced to move into our grandmother's house in southern Tehran, where we lived for the next few years until the revolution started. It was a traditional part of town filled with bazaars and narrow streets lined with children playing hopscotch and old folks drinking tea in the folding chairs they brought out at sunset. As a small child, I loved those streets.

My mother worked six days a week at Revlon, so she needed someone to watch us at home. In Iran, people don't hire babysitters: family members help out with care of the children. But my mother didn't trust any of her siblings. One brother, whom I adored, was a heroin addict. Another was married to a "dark witch," who supposedly peed in people's water jars to bind them with spells. The oldest sister was married to an angry lecher, who, I learned later, had made many passes at my mother.

That left Maman Bozorg as our only caretaker. However, arthritis had given her such a bad limp that she couldn't keep up with me and my brother. So when she'd go to the store to order groceries for delivery, that meant leaving us at home for hours unattended. As soon as my brother and I were too big to stay in our playpens, Maman started tying us to our beds. We complained at first, but she said, "This is what my mother did to me when I was your age and what I did to your mother." Maman had soft, woven ropes with which she'd bind our small feet together and then fasten them to the posts. That way, we were able to move around a bit, but not far enough to hurt ourselves. My brother always cried when she tied us up, and I copied him by crying too. I wasn't that upset, but I wanted to be like him.

Maman Bozorg always smiled while she tied us up. She sang nice songs to us that she invented while knotting the ropes. I remember one in particular that had the word *azadi*, which means "freedom" in Persian. She sang to us, calling us "little birds that want to be free." Every time she finished, she kissed us and promised she'd return quickly, so we could fly again. I liked thinking of myself as a songbird, repeating her songs and taking flight.

Years later, when I told this story to my fellow students in social work school, I was surprised by their horror. Maman's actions had always made sense to me, even if I didn't like them. She was an old woman with arthritis, after all, just trying to get groceries so she could feed us. And at the same time, I know there was no excuse for her tying us up. When I think of all the difficulty I've had staying in relationships, my relentless fear of being "tied down," I can see the deeper damage those knots around my little feet inflicted on me.

My brother couldn't talk until he was five. Before then, I was the one who talked for him and translated the noises and syllables he used to express himself. I was the only one who could decipher his mumbles. My mother, who was impatient to understand what her son was communicating, used to reward me with candy when I explained the meaning of his sounds.

I quickly realized my position of power and began to tell my mother that my brother wanted ice cream and to go to the park, when actually I wanted those things. He just wanted to be held by her and would scream louder when he saw what I was doing, but since I remained the link in the conversation, my actions always worked out for me.

My mother and Maman Bozorg were concerned about my brother's inability to form words. Sometimes they talked among themselves and my mother would cry on Maman Bozorg's shoulders, saying, "Why is this happening to my son?" The two were so distressed that they didn't see the other talents he had, talents only I knew about. For example, my brother had enormous patience and persistence for a kid his age. Once tying us up became an established practice, he gave up crying and began to study Maman Bozorg's knots. After she left, he would spend hours figuring out how to loosen the knots and slip free. I would only briefly try to untie myself, but when I saw how hard it was for my little fingers, I would quickly move into singing and living in my bird world. It was so simple: all I had to do was sing those songs of freedom, and before I knew it, I was gone, flying up and over the narrow streets of Tehran.

I would fly over the tall Tabrizi trees on my favorite street, Vali Aser. The trees arched over the street from both sides, their branches intertwining and creating a tall crown of leaves that hung above the parked cars. The sunlight shone through the leaves, creating a vivid array of oranges, yellows, and reds, which lit the workers passing below. On either side of this street a qanat carried fresh water down from the nearby mountains to all the trees. On sunny days, lovers would rest in the shade of those trees, cooling their feet in the fresh, flowing water.

I remember the day my brother finally figured out how to untie Maman Bozorg's knots. Before leaving, she had opened the windows next to our beds. "So you can watch the other kids play," she said, putting on a colorful chador that covered her from head to toe in a red flower pattern.

"Aaaaooooooeeeeee," my brother yelled, flapping his arm in the air. "Don't leave us here, take us with you," I translated.

"He just said all that?" Maman Bozorg was puzzled.

"Yes he did," I replied confidently. I knew at that young age that the words "my brother wants" got me things, whereas "I want" got me nothing.

"Well, when you get older, I won't have to tie you up anymore," she replied. She finished the last knot and got up to leave.

I sat on the bed near the open windows and listened to the sounds of children outside and smiled. I was so captivated by my daydream that I didn't hear Maman leave. But then I heard my brother yelling. "Neeeee aaaa aaaammm," he wailed. He had a strange look in his eyes.

"What's with you?" I asked him.

His next set of mumbles told me that he'd just figured out how to undo the knots. He began to slowly work the ropes off his feet. He was determined, tongue hanging out of the side of his mouth, totally focused on his mission. I lost interest in what he was doing and went back to my bird songs. This time, I saw myself flying through the blue sky. There were other children flying with me, too. I held their hands, and we laughed as we flapped our wings. There was also a woman in a rainbow-colored dress leading our flight across the treetops. All the other children seemed to like her. *The Rainbow Woman must be their teacher*, I thought. Down below, we saw a forest and a mountain with sharp rocks where children were playing. I felt scared.

Something split inside me. I could hear voices talking, as though in my ear. They seemed at first like a very loud echo, and it frightened me how close they were. They were me, but not me. Or at least, they were separate from me. Gradually, they started to come into focus, and I realized that they wanted to be my friends, unlike the kids down on the street below.

Come hide with us in the House of Stone. There are nice children there and plenty of hugs and ice cream. Come with us, or else go back. But you can't stay here, in between. If you stay in between, you'll get lost and never find your way.

I turned to find my brother on my bed, screaming and shaking me awake.

"Yaaaakhkhaaa khkhooobbbbbbeeeeeee," he screamed, laughing as he held the untied ropes in the air. I looked down and realized that he had freed me too, no doubt while I had been flying with my friends through the forest.

"How did you do that?" I asked him.

He smiled and raised the ropes into the air again before throwing them on the floor. He then jumped down from my bed, landing on the Shirazi rug below and continuing to jump up and down. I joined him on the floor, though my feet felt weak from being tied up. I wanted to make an effort because I knew this was important. After a few minutes, though, we heard Maman Bozorg entering the front yard. My brother bounced back into his bed like a beam of light and wrapped the ropes back around his feet. I, on the other hand, didn't make it in time.

"Maman is back with a snack!" my grandmother called out.

"*Salaam*, Maman," I said, trying to get my feet up over the edge of the bed. "How did you get out?" she asked me with surprise. "I must have forgotten to tie you today. Oh well, let's have a bite to eat!"

I was only four, but I will always remember that day as the day I learned how to leave my body.

I still know how to leave my body, but I can't travel as far anymore. Sometimes when I'm arguing with someone or riding in a car and the driver suddenly swerves, I find myself looking at myself from a few feet away, observing my body with curiosity. That's how I know I'm detaching. I remind myself, "Stay here. My job now is to stay, not go." But sometimes, I let myself linger in that place of observation. After all, if I'm there, there's probably some lesson I need to learn.

Neither my brother nor I remember ever seeing our parents together, except in court a few years later, in the summer before I was in first grade, when they started a custody battle. The judge was sympathetic to my father from the start, as most judges in Iran are, but my mother put up a fight that probably left the judge wondering whether his verdict was worth the headache. My mother is known for her screams, which are capable of changing the weather. I remember her facing down the judge, as the stenographers held their ears and everyone sat nervously on the edge of their seats. I kept watching my father, waiting to see what he would do. He didn't do anything. He looked scared and kept his head down. From time to time, he would look at me and try to smile.

"Do you know how it feels to push two babies out from between your legs?" my mother asked the judge. She seemed to think it was her turn to cross-examine him.

"I don't," the judge admitted.

"So then you have no idea what you are talking about," she said. "You just side with him"—here she pointed at my father—"because he's a man."

The judge apparently had enough of my mother, and he gave my father short-term custody over both my brother and me. We were to see my mother only on weekends, which in Iran means Thursdays and Fridays.

We left the courthouse and stepped out into the brutal Tehran summer heat. I watched some mothers and daughters passing in colorful blouses and bell-bottoms. They held hands, something my mother only did with my brother. I felt a pain in the center of my chest and started to feel myself drifting. Suddenly, a big mountain rose up in front of me, and embedded in it was a little house made of granite. I heard voices of children asking me to go inside.

I turned to look for my mother, and the mountain and house vanished. My father was there instead and took my hand. He was holding my brother with his other hand. My mother saw this, ran over to us, and grabbed each of our free hands. Then she began to pull, and did he, as though we were made of rubber. I used to wonder if my long arms were the result of that day, of all that pulling.

As a young child, I didn't know my father very well. I only remember meeting him in court and a few other times when he came over to Maman Bozorg's house with gifts. I remember finding the word "Baba," which means "father" in Persian, sort of strange. The only men I knew were my mother's brothers. But I was happy to know my baba because he gave me nice gifts: skirts, shirts, and pretty shoes. He seemed fun and his eyes lit up like stars when he saw me, the same way my mother looked when she saw my brother.

After that first visit to court, when Baba got short-term custody, my brother and I moved in with him in his parents' house in midtown Tehran. I liked living with him because he would always tell us stories before bed that sometimes he made up and sometimes he read from a book. I couldn't wait to grow up and learn to read. My brother also developed more verbally and started talking, as though he never had a speech problem. Life was good. I liked my father's parents better than Maman

Bozorg, though I was scared to say so. I called my father's mother Maman Moneer and his father Baba Bozorg. Maman Moneer was a teacher and Baba Bozorg was a sugar salesman.

I also had three uncles on my father's side. One lived in America, and the other two lived in Iran with us in Maman Moneer's house. They were all single and younger than my dad, and so they were always around to play with. One of my uncles, Afshin, was a year younger than my father. He was an animator and saw everything as cartoons. He even set up an animation office in the house. All his friends were artists and came over to make art. My brother and I loved drawing with them. Afshin made short films for Iranian TV, and my brother and I became his main stars.

My father was not into the arts. He was a revolutionary, which is to say he didn't work at all. He had friends over all the time, and they talked about a democratic government where people would rule the country in place of the shah.

"Why don't people like the shah?" I asked my father one day as he drove me to school.

"Because he doesn't care about poor people."

"Why are there poor people?"

"Because the shah makes sure the rich ones get all the opportunities. They go to good schools, get better jobs, and live in better homes."

"That's not fair," I said, though in fact I wasn't exactly sure what he meant.

"Yes, everyone deserves a chance. That's why the people are mad at the shah."

He paused and then pointed out the car window. "Do you see how those beautiful mountains surround the whole city?"

"Yes, Baba," I said. "I see the mountains."

"Tehran is like a big bowl in the valley of these mountains. The poor people live at the bottom of the bowl, and rich people live at the top. The rich people live close to the mountains, where they can get fresh air."

"What's wrong, then?" I wasn't quite following his lecture.

"Well, only rich people get the fresh air. The air stays dirty in the bottom of the bowl, and the people who live there get sick easily. Our sewage system empties out into their neighborhoods. Their children get diseases and miss school often. You know what happens to kids who miss school?"

"Yes," I said. "They don't go to the next grade. Is that why people are mad at the shah?

My father laughed. "Yes," he said, "but there are so many other reasons too."

We arrived at school. He pulled the car up to the big metal doors that marked the main entrance to Parvin Elementary. He offered me both of his cheeks to kiss, just as he always did when saying goodbye.

I have mixed feelings about the idealism of my father and his generation. On the one hand, I wanted so much to be his revolutionary daughter. But I also can't help feeling as though he lived in a cloud at the top of one of the mountains outside Tehran he was telling me about. When I look at photographs of Iran before the revolution he'd wanted so much, there's so much color in them, so much life. And after: only gray. My father would say, tears in his eyes, "And then our revolution was stolen from us"—but couldn't he have seen it coming, that big sweep of gray dust that settled over everything and clogged our eyes and throats? Even as a child, I sensed his magical thinking. It sometimes made me tempted to tell him about the House of Stone. But I thought better and didn't.

2

RED

I'm Red. In the House of Stone, people don't use their given names. Here, they are called only by their favorite colors. I claimed Red because it's the strongest color in the rainbow. Some people think it's a color for adults, but I got here first, so it's mine, even though I'm only seven.

There are many of us, and we all have our own rooms. Mine has a brightly painted red door and a bed that floats. To be honest, I don't spend much time in my room, because I'd rather be where my siblings are: at the center of the house, where there's a firepit and stained-glass windows that let in magical light in the afternoons. These windows are illustrated with all of our futures, which we can't understand yet, but when the sun shines through them, incredible pictures of faraway places and happy times are projected all over the room, like a movie happening everywhere at once. There's warmth in every corner.

Did I mention our House is inside a mountain? From outside, the windows are disguised to look like part of the mountain. This is so no one who hasn't gained permission to enter our House can know where it is or see it. But from within our House, you can see out across the forest, with its thousand shades of pine green and pea green and emerald green, all the way to the other side, where there's a volcano.

No one in the House needs food to survive. If you want something—ice cream or pickles or even costumes for the plays we put on—it comes floating down to you from the big crystal chandelier above. It's all free. But you pay a big price to gain admission here: something really bad must have happened to you. Something bad, but nothing that was your fault. That's the only rule, and everyone has to follow it.

This is a safe house. But outside it are a few things that scare us. There's a volcano, which sometimes spits fire. There's also a witch who put a spell on the volcano and gained control of it. At night, she turns into an owl and flies around the forest. She claims to protect it, but if she ever found our House, she would destroy it and cut off our feet. We don't trust her.

When I first came to the House of Stone, the housekeepers brought me a wooden box and told me to put my memories into it. Of course, I didn't give them everything. I put in a few memories of being hurt by people who were supposed to love me. I took some old screams from out of my throat and slid them into the dark, warm box. It felt like a relief to put them away.

Sometimes people in the House of Stone fight over who owns a memory. It can be hard to tell whose story it is once it's locked away in the box. Mostly we all get along, though, because we all know we have something important to share.

Once in a while, three moons will rise in the sky and stay there many nights, bringing light to the whole forest. We see them through the skylight of our House and know it's time for one of us to get a memory back and make the journey once again to the outer world, where all memories come from. No one really wants to make the journey because it can be scary, but it's important for us not to forget the outer world completely. So we draw straws to see whose turn it will be.

Each of us makes the journey a little differently. One of us walks through a wall of moss. Another goes into a cave. I just blink my eyes a lot. It's a great honor to be chosen, but also scary for some. I'm not scared, though. I've made the journey back and forth from the other world to the House many times. I'm little, but I know a lot. If you stick with me, you won't get lost.

3

CHILDREN OF
THE REVOLUTION

In 1978, people were starting to unite in all the big cities of Iran. Everyone talked about freedom, social justice, equality, and unity. It seemed as though everyone was holding secret meetings in their homes. Maman Moneer also held meetings in her house, where my uncles and their friends joined up with my dad. I had just turned seven when the revolution started to happen. It was an exciting time, even for little children. Everyone seemed to have the same ideas and say the same things. Thousands of people came out daily to show their dissatisfaction with the shah and his regime. They wanted democracy.

I, like so many Iranians, still hold the word "revolution" as somewhat positive—sort of like a parent you want to respect, yet who has let you down in so many ways. When I think of that time, my heart leaps up with joy, but as I play the years forward, I see only devastation and heartbreak.

My dad took my brother and me to demonstrations in Tehran. He taught us about unity and fighting for our rights. I wasn't sure what he meant, but I loved the attention I received from the demonstrators. My dad would put me on his shoulders so I could see the copious crowds on Taleqani Street. I felt like a queen. Others would grab my brother and put him on their shoulders too. All the people acted as though we were one big family. Even the gun-toting police who watched the crowd seemed friendly. Demonstrators sang and asked the policemen to join us. They never did, but they always smiled. I remember a lady offering white tulips to the policemen.

"Don't use bullets, use flowers," she said. One of the police smiled at me. I gave him the peace sign. I knew adults always got happy when children gave them the peace sign.

One demonstration was different, however. There were a lot of people in the street shouting louder than usual. My dad held my hand more tightly, nervously. This time, the police pointed their guns at the people in the crowd. They had masks on and wore thick vests. My dad looked down at my brother and me and said in a commanding voice, "We're leaving as fast as we can. Don't stop, and don't look back."

We turned and walked quickly through the crowd. I felt bodies pushing from behind me, people stepping on my feet. With a trickle and then a rush, everyone started to run in the same direction. I felt a surge of energy in my chest, my heart clanging along with everyone else's, a chorus of gongs I can hear still. Then loud bangs from up close. People lying down on the ground, as though asleep, with red splotches on them. Red splotches on my arms too. Was I shot? "Run and don't look back," I said to myself and managed to break through the crowd.

It was only when I reached the edge of the boulevard that I realized I had no idea where my dad or brother was. Then I heard a voice:

You need to turn here. The owls can follow a straight path.

I turned onto a quiet street and felt myself lift off the ground.

Fly. Get away from the open ground.

I noticed I wasn't flying, however, but was in the arms of a young man who stood in a doorway. He dragged me into his house, a terrified look on his face.

"Let me go!" I cried.

"No, you have to stay calm. It's okay, I'm a friend."

"My brother and dad are in the crowd." I was crying loudly now.

"What was your dad thinking, taking a kid to a demonstration?" he frowned. He was breathing hard. "Are you hurt?" He gestured at the blood on my arms.

"No," I said. "But I want to go home now."

"Of course you do," he said, leading me into the courtyard of his building. "There's a curfew, though. That means no one's allowed to go anywhere after dark. Where do you live, anyway?"

In the light of the courtyard, I could see he was a tall, thin young man with long black hair. His black T-shirt had the logo of a fist on the front. He kept flicking his bangs out of his face.

"Near Parvin Elementary," I replied. That was all I knew. I could find my way if I was near my school. But I didn't know my house address.

"Wow, that's quite a walk. Okay, I'll take you tomorrow, as soon as it's safe."

A woman yelled down from the balcony. "What are you doing in the yard, Majid? Come up!"

"That's my mother," Majid said.

"There's tea!" the woman yelled again. Majid took my hand and helped me up the flight of steps. Each step held a little flower pot with a few narcissus plants in it.

"Where did you find this little girl?" Majid's mother asked him when we reached the top.

I don't remember the rest of their conversation. There was a table covered with sweets, pistachios, and dried fruits, which I gobbled down right before immediately passing out on their divan.

In the morning, Majid took me back to school and then walked beside me as I showed him the way to my house. We walked in silence for a bit. Then he asked me, trying to make conversation, "So what do you want to do when you grow up?"

"I'm going to have two husbands," I told him. He burst out laughing.

"Why do you want that?" he asked.

"My father says that important and powerful men sometimes have two wives. I'm going to be important and powerful too."

He smiled and didn't say anything.

When we arrived, my grandparents first yelled at Majid, then gave him a big hug for bringing me. My grandmother couldn't stop crying; she obviously thought I'd been shot. Baba Bozorg held me in his arms and wouldn't put me down.

"Are her father and brother okay?" Majid asked.

"Yes, they're in the living room. Please come meet them," Maman Moneer said.

"Thanks," he said, "but I have to head back." He started to leave but turned just before he reached the door. "Is her name really Fire?"

My grandfather nodded. Majid smiled, flashed me a peace sign, and left. I never saw him again, but I always thought of him as my first love.

My mother was frightened by the madness she saw in the streets and the loud "Allahu Akbar" chants coming from the rooftops. Each night she cried. In the mornings, I often heard her moan, "What a horrible time for a single mother to raise kids alone!" She wasn't really raising us alone, of course—my brother and I only visited her on weekends—but she refused to mention our father or his role in our lives.

Tehran was a scary place in those days, and people made sure they got home before the sun went down. Snipers were everywhere, and it was never clear when or where shots would come from. One day, though, my mother forgot to get bread for our evening meal. It was well after dark when we realized this.

"I'll go, Mommy," my brother offered.

I was proud of my brother for being brave, but my mother scooped him up with a gesture that said she wasn't going to let him leave.

"Let me go, Mommy," I offered. "I run really fast."

Maman Bozorg sat up in her chair with a panicked look. "You're not letting a seven-year-old go, right?" There was a silence as everyone waited to see what would happen next.

"She runs fast," my mother said and turned away.

I opened the door and faced the night air. Behind me, I heard my mother tell my brother, "I could never bear to lose you."

I felt a tug inside, something drawing me toward a place in my mind where I was wanted and chosen. But I also knew that, despite her coldness, my mother did need me. I made up my mind that I would be her favorite after all. I would become even more of a boy than my brother, bulletproof, fast as lightning, resolute in his mission to return with bread.

I changed course and stepped back inside. I went upstairs to my brother's room and exchanged my skirt for a pair of his pants. In those days, my grandmother kept our hair very short, so I knew my disguise would work. Then I stepped back onto the street.

I ran through the dark, hearing the crackling sounds of gunfire from rooftops not too far off. I made two lefts, until I found myself in a wide, empty street. The air was thinner than usual. I heard a loud sound nearby and inspected my body. There was no blood, but I felt something damp and cold between my legs:

I'd peed myself. When I made my final turn and reached the *noonvaii* (baker's shop), I saw he was closing for the night.

"Boy, what on earth are you doing out on the street?" the baker yelled. I was pleased that my short haircut had fooled him. The delightful smell of baked bread made me feel safe. The tanoor oven built into the wall had no fire in it: he was clearly shutting the place down. At that moment, I realized I'd forgotten money. I pointed desperately at the few loaves still on his shelf.

"It's all cold," he said. "Take whatever you want and get out of here quick."

I scooped up a few *barbari* loaves and ran proudly through the night, a soldier returning victorious from battle. As I neared home, arms full of cold bread, I heard a voice inside say:

Don't act too much like a boy. She'll figure it out. I'm here, and I will always protect you. But you have to keep our secret.

I turned around, but no one was there, so I went inside. I felt happy. I felt guided by something beyond me, something wise. I did as the voice suggested, put my skirt back on, and walked into the living room proudly holding the bread. I was pleased to catch a glint of tears in my mother's eyes.

It wasn't that my mother didn't love me. She did, but her love always came with the unspoken judgment that she would have loved me more if I were a boy. It was around that time that I started to ask my brother regularly for his hand-me-downs. It was also around that time that I started to realize that part of me really was male. Being able to accept that fully, however, would take many years.

My mother soon found a measure of protection in my soon-to-be stepfather, a successful clothing distributor who sold to small shops in Tehran. He told her he was willing to take care of my brother and me. According to my mother, he was also rich. Pretty soon, they were married and he moved into Maman

Bozorg's house. My mother enjoyed the fact that he brought her jewelry each time he came home from work. She was happy to have a man around.

The revolution ended in February of 1979. There were still so many blood stains on the streets. I used to collect bullet shells for my school art projects. I was no longer so afraid of dead people; I'd seen so many lying around. I had to travel to other countries before I realized that stepping over corpses isn't most people's reality.

In April, Ayatollah Khomeini replaced the shah and declared Iran to be an Islamic Republic. A cloud of fear started to form around everyone I knew. They kept saying their revolution and hope for democracy were "stolen" and that there was no longer any *azadi*—the freedom Maman Bozorg used to sing about. People didn't sing any more, either on TV or in the streets. Everyone talked about moving to England or France, but no one ever seemed to go. I didn't know it then, but the borders were already closed.

Newspapers showed pictures of executed men. "Friends of the Shah," a headline said. At school, teachers separated boys and girls. I couldn't enter the building with my brother anymore. People started to dress differently. Women wore scarves and long shirts that covered their arms and hips. One weekend, when I was at my mother's, she came home crying that she'd been shamed at work for wearing a skirt. "People are saying I'll lose my job if I don't wear a veil," she cried to my stepfather.

"That's true," my stepfather said. "You know, I've been thinking you should stop working entirely. It's a new era. Besides, I make good money and you can make the house. Other men shouldn't see you anyway."

I was glad to hear him say that. Personally, I wanted my mother to lose her job so she'd have to stay home with me. But his words didn't go over well with her at all.

"Oh, is that right?" she said, her face turning from irritation to fury. "So you're one of *them* now?"

He started to back down. "Not at all, my love. I just want to protect you."

"You just want to make sure strangers don't look at me."

She was right, and yet he won. My mother soon got pregnant and resigned from her decade-long job at Revlon. The day she resigned, my stepfather came home with a gift for her. I assumed it would be more jewelry, or another fancy purple sweater. Instead, it was a solid-black chador that would cover her from head to toe.

"You're joking, right?" my mother said. "The shah leaves, and I should dress like the Prophet's mother?"

But the next day, I saw her trying it on in front of the mirror.

Sometimes I see how much I'm like my mother. We're both spirited and rebellious. And we also both know how to surrender to change, often by allowing an ordinary object, like a veil or a hat or a new haircut, to transform us into someone different. We fight and fight and then, when we can't fight any more, we become. See, it isn't so bad. Or maybe it is.

Now dressed in a chador, my mother started to pray and talk about going to Qom, the most religious city in Iran, where my grandmother was also from.

"Let's spend the summer there," my mother said to my stepfather. "We can pray to the saints. They'll bless our marriage and new child." She patted her big round belly.

I never liked Qom. The sun was always boiling and the tap water tasted salty. I couldn't see the women's noses or mouths, as they covered even their faces in black. This frightened me. But my previous experiences were nothing compared to what happened in Qom that summer of 1979, when we stayed at the house of Maman Bozorg's cousin, a very well-respected religious teacher there.

"He's a saint," Maman Bozorg said about the teacher. "You have to be nice to him or bad things will happen."

"His invitation is a blessing," my mother chimed in.

The saint's house was full of children and people carrying around plates of rich food: duck, pomegranate stews, eggplant dishes. I enjoyed playing with the children, but I didn't like it when the adults would leave to visit some shrine or other, because then we had to stay in the basement, where the saint would watch us. He had a hairy nose, fat belly, a walleye, and a tongue that flicked in and out of his mouth like a lizard's. I wondered whether all saints were ugly and whether they then became beautiful in heaven.

The saint set us up with arts and crafts in the basement, on a table that had woodworking materials and paper for drawing. The basement had doors that led to a large garden, but the children were scared to go there. There were demons in the garden, they said.

A few days later, while I was drawing a tree, the saint came and took a little restless boy by the hand. The boy didn't want to go, but the saint told the boy to look into his eyes, and the boy put his head down and followed the saint into the garden of demons.

The saint came back a little later without the boy. Then he went out again; then he came back. I asked what happened to the boy. "Don't be nosy," the saint said. A few hours later, the little boy returned, but he wasn't restless anymore. He didn't talk to anyone and sat staring at the wall. I tried to get him to color with me, but he turned his back to me. I wondered if the demons had stolen his soul.

A few days later, the saint came for me. I didn't want to go, but he held my shoulder and said, "You don't want to fight me." He led me through one of the doors, out into the garden, where birds were singing. *This isn't so bad*, I thought. *Maybe I'll see the Rainbow Woman again.*

At the edge of the garden, there were some outdoor rooms and outhouses. The saint opened the door of a shed and pushed me in. "I'll be back soon," he said. As my eyes adjusted to the darkness, I noticed that the walls were covered with cockroaches. I shook the handle of the door, but that just made the roaches fly around the room and into my hair. I screamed. From behind the door, I heard the saint's voice say, "Shush. Be a good girl. If you move too much the roaches will get you." I promised I'd be good.

Are you scared? I can hide you, but you'll have to leave right now. You don't have to feel bad. Ever. Please don't stay here.

I looked around and then down. I was flying high above Vali Asr Street. There were other children flying too, laughing as they flapped their arms. Then everything got very bright and still.

I don't know how long I was in that shed, but when the saint returned, I was lying on the floor with roaches on top of me. He told me that a lot of my sins were gone now. "This room purifies," he said. "But one more thing has to be done." I took his hand and followed him, checking as I walked to see if any bugs were still in my shirt or pants. He took me to another part of the basement and put me on a table face down. He took off my pants and told me I was good. Then he spit on my back and I felt something enter my spine, till I thought it would snap, and all I wanted to do was number two, but I couldn't. The pain was so enormous that I felt the wall in front of me start to split open. In the crack of the wall, I saw a beautiful woman with long black hair and a long black dress holding her hand out to me.

My name is Black. Come take my hand. Crawl through the crack in the stone. Otherwise you'll die.

I looked over her shoulder. In the distance was a misty forest, filled with trees that had human faces and arms that looked like magic wands.

I put my hand against the wall. To my amazement, it went through, as though the stone were made of water. Then I felt Black's strong hand gently pull me through the wall, through a path between the trees, and then finally, through the door of the House of Stone.

I was overjoyed. I can get there even from *here*!

Children were gathered around the firepit. They stopped what they were doing and came over to say hello. "I know them," I said to myself.

Of course you do. They're always here, waiting for you to join.

I saw colored butterflies standing guard outside the doorway of the house. Their faces were beaming.

Those are real. The butterflies, not the roaches. Remember.

But then, sadly, I was back in the basement. I looked up and saw that the saint was fixing a lamp. He saw me staring and said, "If you tell anyone what happened today, your mother and grandmother will burn in hell forever." Then he smiled and told me again I was a good girl.

Back in the basement, he brought all of us watermelon and had the kids sit down to eat it, but the kids who had already been to the garden of demons wouldn't participate. One boy kept brushing his arms, as if there were something crawling on them. Another girl was terrified by the black watermelon seeds and started mumbling about bugs. I was happy to be out of the garden, however, and ate heartily. I scooped up as many watermelon seeds as I could to save for later.

The saint's wife came down and said our parents had returned. My mother and Maman Bozorg were happy to see me, and asked how my day was. I couldn't speak. "What do you have in your hand?" my mother asked. I showed her the seeds. She told me to put them into the trash, but as I walked away, I stuffed them up my nose instead. I'm not sure why I did that: maybe to seal myself shut so nothing else could get in me. Some of the seeds fell out, but I could feel some others find a home in my head. *Maybe I'll grow a garden*, I thought. *That way, Rainbow Woman and Black will know where to find me again.*

But a few days later, a bad smell started to come from my nose. Everyone who tried to pick me up and hug me smelled the rotten stench and put me down right away. I felt victorious.

No one could figure out where the smell was coming from. My mother made me change my underwear and brush my teeth, over and over. Nothing helped, till my brother decided to drink a bottle of iodine that was sitting in the bathroom. To this day, I'm still not sure why he did that. Since we came to Qom, he seemed as sad as me.

We had to rush him to the hospital to have his stomach pumped. There, a nurse realized I had watermelon seeds rotting in my nose. "Not rotting," I told her. "Growing." But they told me they were going to have to perform surgery. They took me into a different room and put me out. Later, after I woke, I noticed I had a little line on the side of my nose. They released my brother and me the next day. My mother was distraught. "Why is everything going wrong in the most holy place on earth?" she wailed.

I started washing my hands a lot. Sometimes I would spend a full hour at the sink, till my skin looked like little raisins. My brother started to be afraid of water bugs, even when none were around. Sometimes when he was sleeping, I would find water bugs and put them in his shirt. He would start to pat himself in his sleep, then build up the patting to strong slapping, and then, finally, would wake up screaming.

I'm really, really sorry for doing that to him.

As an adult, I asked my brother so many times whether something had happened to him in Qom, but he would never say. He would just get angry. My fear of roaches never went away, though. Nor did my deep shame at being in the role of a bully. Before, I'd thought that what I longed for was to hurt people the way I had been hurt. But I realized that what I really wanted was for people to know what had happened to me.

As dark as that time was, I still remember how patiently I waited for my mother to give birth and how overjoyed I was when she came home carrying my little sister Ava in a wicker basket. I sat next to that basket for hours, waiting for the baby to open her eyes. When she did and started to cry, my mother let me pick her up, and immediately my baby sister got quiet. My mother smiled approvingly. I marveled at how complete something so small could be and how complete I felt holding her. I felt I'd found something permanent, something that couldn't be destroyed like one of my dolls: a place in my mother's heart.

My father was never the same after the revolution. Perhaps out of guilt for being alive when so many people he knew had died, he married the sister of his dead best friend, a young woman named Afsaneh. That's what my mother told me, at least. Afsaneh was young and pretty, and always was nice to me. I knew her before my father married her, because she was one of the animators who came to work with my uncle Afshin.

I liked going to Afshin's animation studio because it had so many crayons, watercolors, and even oil paints. Every time I went there, I drew another part of the forest surrounding the House of Stone. People asked about my paintings and were always surprised by how much I had to tell them about the place I drew. But no one knew that the House was real. Except me.

My mother despised Afsaneh. She believed Afsaneh had always been after my dad, even before the divorce. When it became clear that my father and Afsaneh were serious, there was talk among my father's family of sending my brother and me to live with our mother permanently, to give the new couple space to make their own family.

There were other reasons too. My father started drinking heavily at that time, and he could be violent. His smiles disappeared and his star-like gaze turned to empty space. He became a different man: short-tempered, discontented. In the year following the revolution, he was constantly snapping at my brother and me for things that used to make him smile. He smacked my brother for pronouncing a big word wrong, where once he would have rewarded him for trying. He began to hit us when we came home late from school, didn't do our homework on time, or didn't tie our shoelaces fast enough.

His beatings replaced our bedtime stories. My brother and I hid when we heard his footsteps. My father was never as mean to me as he was to my brother, and my brother yearned for our mother's touch and kept crying for her. This made my father even angrier. Once, as my brother was in the middle of one of his wailing sessions, my father said, "If you don't stop, I'll get my belt." My brother didn't stop, so my father went into the other room.

I felt so bad for my brother. I didn't want him to get even more hurt. So I did something I swore I wouldn't do: I told him about the House of Stone.

"I know how to leave," I said. "Listen. You press your thumbs into your eye sockets and put pressure there till it really hurts. Then you can go to the other side with me, where I have many friends." I showed him how to do it. "Like this. Now let's go behind the couch before Baba finds us."

We crouched behind the couch and put pressure on our eyeballs. I opened my eyes once to check on my brother. His thumbs were in the right position. I sensed him with me, entering my secret world.

Look at all these people carrying you on their shoulders. They throw you in the air and catch you again. Black is here too, watching from afar.

I looked down: I had on my brother's hand-me-down shorts, which I always wore. Then I looked again: my shorts had become the robes of a prince.

You are royalty here. People bow down and welcome you into their circle. They throw flowers. You are very, very important.

"Didn't I tell you how beautiful this is?" I said to my brother. "Do you like it here?" I asked as I blinked a few times. I wanted to take him all the way to the inside of the House of Stone. But something was wrong, because I realized I was back in my father's house, on the floor.

You can't bring him here. He isn't invited. I'm your real brother now.

My brother's shirt was ripped, and he looked sad. My royal robes were gone too. "I couldn't do it," he cried.

"Yes, you did," I assured him. "You were there with me. I saw you, I swear."

I tried to get up from the floor but my body hurt. I saw my father sitting across from us on the couch, exhausted. He was crying softly and muttering something about never hitting us again. I had no idea what he meant. I didn't remember being beaten, though my body ached all over. I thought to myself: *I have to tell the crowd not to throw me so high up into the air next time.*

"You're stupid," my brother said. "He hit us and you know it."

Eventually my father left the room. My brother turned to me. "Get your bag. We're leaving," he said.

"Where to?" I wasn't sure whether to take him seriously.

"Maman Bozorg's," he said.

"But that's too far," I said. "We'll get lost. We're just kids." I remembered that it used to take my father a long time with his car to get to Maman Bozorg's house.

"I know the way," my brother said. "I have money for the taxi. But you can't get crazy, Atash. I need your help."

I put on a different pair of pants and took some of the money I had hidden inside a rag doll. I followed my brother out of the house. We had to take many different cabs to get to Maman Bozorg's place. Each taxi driver gave us a hard time about traveling without our parents. My brother assured them that our parents were waiting at the other end and that he had money to pay them. One fellow seemed convinced and took us as far as his zoning regulations allowed. The trip was so long that it took us three more taxis after that one to get there.

When we finally got to Maman Bozorg's, we realized there was, in fact, no one home. My brother seemed agitated and started nervously pulling at the collar of his shirt.

"Maman Bozorg must be up with Mommy in Ramsar." I stared at him in disbelief, because Ramsar was by the Caspian Sea, a whole day's travel away. "Yes," he continued, "I remember now. She said she was planning to go there for a month."

"A month?" I was starting to get scared.

"Don't worry," he said, in a tone of voice that made me very worried. "I know how to break in."

"I'm hungry," I said.

"There's food in the fridge," he said. "Now listen. Maman's doors are locked, but there's a wall beneath her kitchen window. I'm going to climb it. I'll open the door for you after."

I don't know how he fit through that tiny square window, but he did. A few minutes later he was at the front door and let me in.

"We're going to live here till Mommy comes back," he announced.

Later that afternoon, I heard the doorbell ring. My brother and I were taking a nap after having a delicious dinner of hotdogs, dates, and cookies. I went to the little square window my brother had climbed through and looked outside. My father and his two brothers Amin and Afshin were standing with their motorcycles in the street. They saw me too.

"Oh my God, they're here!" Amin shouted happily. I waved at them. They waved back. Without thinking, I climbed through the window and stood on the edge of the wall. I wanted to show off our window trick to them.

"Don't!" my brother shouted from the kitchen. "They're here to take us back."

But I was happy they'd found us. My father was speechless, staring up at his little seven-year-old girl balancing on the edge of the second-floor ledge. My uncles both were standing below, holding their arms up for me to jump into. I wanted to jump, but every time I was about to leap, my brother would yell, "Don't!"

I was confused. Eventually, though, I found my way down into Amin's arms. Afshin picked me up and kissed me. My father was still speechless. At last, he opened his mouth and called to my brother to come out. My brother announced he was staying put.

"If you don't have the keys, Baba, I can go back in through the window and get him," I offered. That made them all laugh.

I didn't want my brother to be left alone. *Everyone has changed*, I thought. *They've all learned their lesson. Now we need to be together.*

"You stay right here," my father said. "He'll come out on his own." It felt like an eternity, but sure enough, after some time, my brother came walking out the front door. He didn't want to be kissed or hugged. My father put his hand on his shoulders, but my brother just pushed it away.

Later, I learned how much effort it had taken them to find us. They'd been to our school, to all our friends' houses, and to several precincts in the city, trying to get information. It was only then that they thought of Maman Bozorg's house. I think it was my father who guessed our location because he remembered how well my brother knew the road back to our mother.

I don't remember my father hitting us again. My brother's plan worked better than my bird flights.

For so long, I thought it was my fault that our parents separated and never seemed to be in a good mood. I thought that, if I just learned to be good enough, I would have my father in my life again. That meant, of course, not showing him what was happening to me on the inside. When he'd catch me talking to myself or staring off into space and ask what I was doing, I'd laugh and say, "Oh nothing." I wouldn't tell him about all the people I saw or the distances I traveled with them.

Soon after the revolution, Iraq invaded Iran and the eight-year war between them began. Within days, Tehran was on fire. Iraqi planes flew over the sky, dropping explosives all over the city and blowing out windows. There were hardly any stores without holes in them, and thieves combed the streets. I often heard adults talking about how this jewelry store or that electronics dealer had been robbed. Even supermarkets weren't safe.

Everyone carried portable radios at all times to make sure they could hear the sirens and have time to take refuge in underground bomb shelters. The sound of sirens used to terrify me, not so much because I feared the bombs, but because I was afraid of getting stepped on when the crowd scattered in panic. At night, Afsaneh lit candles. She taught my brother and me not to use lights because the Iraqi planes would see us and bomb our house. Now, she was the one who held her puffy, pregnant belly and talked to her unborn child, trying to comfort her. Back then, I used to think it was the smell of explosives that made her vomit so much.

One night, when I was asleep, my father came into the room my brother and I shared and woke us up. "Get up now! We have to evacuate!" He had a cigarette lighter in his hand that he used as a torch to shine our way through the darkness. I could hear the sound of planes louder than ever, as though they were right above our building. When we finally made it into the hallway, I saw neighbors crying and running down the stairs. A deafening sound shook us. Windows shattered. After that, everything moved in slow motion. Everyone got down on the ground and held their heads. I shut my eyes and crossed over to the other side.

Do you know what these loud sounds are? They're fireworks for our special celebration. People are dancing beneath the tree leaves and splashing water from a nearby spring on each other. Let me splash you too.

When I opened my eyes, I saw it was my father putting water on my forehead.

"Everything's okay, sweetie. Don't worry." He was crying as he mumbled the words. "Where are the planes?" I asked. "Are they gone?"

"Yes," he said. "The bombs didn't actually hit us, just nearby." He helped me put on a new pair of pants. Apparently, I'd peed myself. After I was cleaned up, he took me to my room and tucked me into bed. My brother was already there, almost asleep.

"Do all the children go to sleep with the sound of bombs?" my brother asked.

"I don't know," I said. "But the people dancing in the forest were really beautiful."

"Why are you like this?" he said. "What's wrong with you?"

People did the most unpredictable things in those days: someone would come up to another person on the street and punch that person without reason; hit-and-runs became common. One day, on my way to school, I saw a huge crowd forming a big circle near a street intersection. People were shouting things about a man who was about to be hanged at the center of the circle. I was scared, but my legs carried me deeper into the crowd. I had to see what was going to happen next. I was little, so I pushed my way between people till I got to the very front of the crowd.

The accused man was enormous. He was wearing dark pants and no shoes. His button-down shirt had ripped sleeves. He had no hair and looked even older than my father. The mob was leading him to a gibbet someone had made from the crane of a construction truck. He fought, swinging his arms, as the mob dragged him on. Then he saw me. I felt my whole body freeze as his gaze locked with mine. He stopped struggling. *Why is he looking at me like that?* I wondered. The sound of my heart was like a gong in my chest. I couldn't turn or blink. It was as though he were begging me to stay or go with him somewhere else.

Another big man came up and put a rope around the accused man's neck and tied his hands behind him. People threw garbage and pitched forward. I felt the hands of adults pushing me aside, and I lost sight of the accused man.

I started to cry. "No, no, no, please let him go!" But no one heard me. I tried to get back into the circle, but there was no way in. Then I heard people yelling, "He's dead! The beast is dead!"

Others joined in the shouting. *"Bacheh-baz-e kasif mord!"* (He's dead! The dirty pedophile is dead!) Then the crowd pushed me even further out, and I couldn't hear or see anything.

In school, I asked my teacher what a pedophile is. The word in Farsi is *bacheh-baz*, which literally means "someone who plays with kids." It sounded like a fun person to me.

"Why would people kill a man who likes to play with kids?" I asked my teacher.

She smiled. "No one would ever want to hurt someone who likes playing with kids." Then I used the word bacheh-baz, and her face lost its color.

"Where did you hear that word?" she said.

"In the street. They hanged the *bacheh-baz*. Will they kill the man in Qom too?"

"No one was hanged, sweetie! Why would anyone kill anyone? Come here." She held me in her lap, caressed my hair, and read to me till it was time to go home.

As a school social worker, I know all too well how many children are abused in their own homes. It only takes a few signs for the alarm bells to go off in me: the smell of a child who has stopped washing, their empty stares, the way a child eats or doesn't eat in the cafeteria, their hypervigilance or total dissociation. To some people, these are pieces of evidence that can be endlessly disputed. But to me, it's not a matter of inference. I have a sixth sense for child abuse, and I won't stop pushing until I find the truth. That's one of the blessings hidden in the curse of being the family scapegoat: the truth of all dysfunction is located in one body—in this case, mine—and with some awareness, that body can become a radar for when abuse is happening.

On the way home after school that day, I saw Siavash, a nineteen-year-old boy with bad acne who only played with kids younger than him. I wondered if Siavash was a *bacheh-baz*.

I always liked Siavash because he looked like Majid, the young man from the demonstration who had saved me. I noticed that Siavash always had lots of sweets and shared them with anyone who wanted them. He played ball with all the younger kids and played the role of coach. But I'd never been introduced to him, so that day, on the way home from school, I walked up to him, told him my name, and mentioned that we were neighbors.

"I never see you around," he said.

"That's because I live with my father one week and my mother the next," I said. "I have two homes, not like ordinary kids."

"I see," he said. "But how do you make friends if you're always moving?"

"I don't have many," I said, feeling myself get sad. "My brother's my only friend."

"It's okay," Siavash said. "I don't have many friends either."

"Why don't you play with people your own age?" I asked.

"Because they're mean," he said.

I looked at him, trying to figure out why that would be. To this day, I never understood why he was terrified of people his own age. When he gave kids candy he always had them sit on his lap, and I remember he moved around a lot underneath them. He tried to get me to sit on his lap too, but I wouldn't. He also tried to get me to go with him behind a car to show me his parts.

"Don't you want to see mine?" he asked.

I told him I'd seen things before.

"Yeah, like what?"

"I promised not to tell anyone."

"Really?" Siavash's eyes widened.

"Yes," I said.

After that conversation, Siavash never tried to get me to come behind a car with him again, though I let him kiss me on the lips a few times. He treated me differently than the other kids, though. With me, he'd talk about how his father would get drunk and try to touch him. I remember feeling very adult-like, sitting there listening to him. I felt sorry for him, and I knew he wasn't going to hurt me. I knew, even then, that when you make connections with people, they have something to lose and will protect you. Sometimes I even stole some food from Afsaneh's kitchen to bring to him. We could hang out in our building's garage for hours, or till I saw my father's car, at which point I'd say goodbye and go upstairs to act as though I'd been studying all afternoon.

I never got caught playing when I wasn't supposed to, but my brother did a lot. It didn't matter which one of us got caught, though; we both would get grounded the same, which for me meant not getting to see Siavash for a while.

"Does Siavash play with you like he does with me?" I asked my brother one day.

"I don't want to talk about it," he said.

I had a lot of bad dreams in those days. The saint from Qom and the hanged man both visited me regularly. The saint gave me a box that I thought was a birthday present, but when I opened it, water bugs flew out, and I woke up screaming. I never told anyone why I screamed. Other nights, I saw the hanged man and tried to save him, but sometimes he would try to kill me first. I always woke up before I died, though. In one dream, he managed to grab me, but some people found us and took me away before he could hurt me. But then I realized that those people were going to take him to the gibbet made from a construction crane, so I said, "He's with me, he's not bad," and they believed me. In another dream, the hanged man became my friend and choked the saint in Qom with my grandmother's ropes. Then we buried him in the garden of demons.

I once told my mother about my dreams. We were on our way to the Tehrani Bazaar. I was trying to keep her attention, but the Tehrani Bazaar is a very distracting place. There are colors everywhere: fiery oranges, reds, greens, yellows, and blues. There are dried fruits, like *anjeer* (figs) and *albaloo* (sour cherries) hanging from the stalls, and there is always the constant screaming of black-market salesmen hawking dollars, diamonds, and gold. As usual, once inside the bazaar, everyone was competing with me for my mother's attention. I didn't know whether this was because they wanted to sell their products or take a closer look at my mother's beautiful face.

"I have fresh fish, caviar, saffron, pistachios!" one man said. "Come in! I have everything a household could need."

He looked quickly at me, and then his gaze lingered on my mother's body, wrapped in a tight-fitting black dress and tiny black headscarf that still revealed most of her hair.

"Mommy," I said, "if the hanged man ends up killing me one night in my dream, will I die in real life?"

My mother kept her gaze on the fishmonger. I wasn't sure if she was smiling to let me or him know she was listening.

"Mommy, are you paying attention?"

But she was. A part of her was always paying attention. And sure enough, one sunny spring morning in court, as she made her petition to take me and my brother to live near the Caspian Sea with her, she repeated every bit of my dream to the judge.

"What kind of father would let his kids see a man be hanged? The poor thing brings her nightmares to me, while he drinks all day and won't watch his children."

And I thought: *What kind of mother lets her daughter be hurt so she can pray?*

The judge was a scrawny old man who peered down at me over his glasses every time my mother mentioned me. I shrank in my seat when he looked my way.

"Let me ask the children how they feel," he said to my mother.

I couldn't answer, of course. I was sobbing the whole time, and the judge couldn't decipher my tears. I wanted to say, "Let me stay with my father," but I was afraid. Besides, I didn't want to lose my brother, so I said nothing.

"Okay," the judge said finally. "You can keep your daughter, and Mr. Yaghmaian can keep his son. That's the most natural way. Sons with fathers and daughters with mothers."

My mother let out a shriek. "I want my son!"

My heart sank. But the judge seemed pleased with his decision and gave my mother only partial custody of my brother and full custody over me. My father didn't make a scene in court. He just took my brother's hand and walked out of the building. My mother chased them into the courtyard and tried to pull my brother from my father. She kissed my brother all over like a hungry dog, as if this was the last time they'd ever see each other. My father picked me up and kissed me goodbye.

"You'll grow up and understand why I have to leave you with your mother," he whispered. But I never understood.

Then my father put me down and started to walk away with my brother, his eyes fixed on the ground.

My mother yelled after him, "I loved you and gave you my soul! Now you are taking my one and only son!" She continued howling for a while. Then she called out to my brother across the courtyard, "Don't worry, I will save you soon."

I looked over at my brother and waved at him. I wondered why my mother loved him so much more than me. He waved back. Then we walked in different directions. As I walked with my mother, our steps started to sink into the ground, and I felt better, knowing I was returning to the House of Stone.

4

BLUE

’m Blue. I’m a boy—a real boy. I came to this forest through a cave from the world beyond, where my body was a girl’s body and they made me wear dresses with puff sleeves. But here, I look like me.

My mother is the ruler of this forest. She calls me “little soldier” and has entrusted me with the mission of tracking down all the little girls here and bringing them to her. My mother doesn’t like girls. She says they’re bad luck and bring danger. I always fail at my mission, however. Each day, I return without any girls and a new excuse. The truth is, I’ve heard what she does to them. She puts snakes in their bellies.

Whenever I return without any girls, my mother gets upset and tells me I’m not her real son. “You’re a fake boy!” she screeches. Then she points upstairs to where her “real son” is lying sick in bed. I’m not allowed to see him, but one of the servants told me once that my mother cut off his feet to keep him from leaving. That’s when I first thought about leaving too.

I didn’t know about the House of Stone until I met Red. I found her in the forest one day. She was following a butterfly down a long dirt path. Her big brown eyes met mine, and I saw how much she looked like me. We had the same bowl-shaped haircut and the same sad smile. When she saw me coming, she said, "Can you hear them calling?" We listened, and I heard a voice, like a schoolteacher's, echoing from far off. "Miss, Miss, where are you?"

"They're looking for you," Red told me.

"I'm not a girl," I said. "I'm a boy. And a soldier."

"Well, I don't think they know that," Red said. "And they're not being very nice."

We listened again to the echo.

"Are you deaf? Or possessed?" the voice said from afar. "There must be something really wrong with you." Then we heard the sounds of students laughing at their teacher's joke.

"You're just hearing the other world," Red said. "Don't let it bother you. When you're here in the forest, no one from the other side can hurt you."

"I'm not a girl in any world," I said again. "I'm a soldier who's been entrusted with bringing all the girls of the forest to my mother."

"How many girls have you brought her so far?" Red asked.

"None," I said. This made Red laugh.

"I could if I wanted to," I said. "I'm a really good soldier. But I don't want to bring her any."

Red didn't say anything. She just looked at me, and I felt she was really trying to be my friend.

"The truth is," I said, staring at my feet, "she hurts them with snakes."

A little teardrop formed in Red's left eye and began to roll down her face. She brushed it off quickly.

"I live in a place where that can't happen," she said at last. "I can show it to you if you like. It's called the House of Stone, and there are lots of nice kids there."

"Do they play soccer?" I asked. I hadn't played soccer in a very long time.

"Yes," Red said. "And we have a special tree that makes rosewater taffy too."

She led me down several winding paths that twisted round and round until I couldn't remember which direction we'd come from. I was also distracted by the fact that all the plants and flowers had eyes. When I stared at them, they'd get shy and blink. But they didn't seem scary to me, just curious. The butterflies also had faces. At some point, a large cat joined us too, as though he were entrusted with the task of leading us somewhere important.

Red stopped us by a hill covered with moss. "Put your hand in," she said. I did, and a door in the hillside opened up. We walked through it and down a narrow rock corridor that opened onto a massive hall filled with chandeliers and lined with entrances to many bedrooms. There were a dozen kids, between seven and seventeen, all sitting around, laughing. At first, I thought they were laughing at me, and I wanted to leave, but I soon realized they were just happy.

"You can have the corner room on the second floor," Red said. "The one with the blue door. Stay as long as you like, but I think your mother is looking for you. She sounds angry."

I listened but couldn't hear anything. "I only hear the kids," I told her. "How do you know?"

"I hear everything," Red said. "Inside and outside. That's my secret power. Everyone who comes to the House has a power. What's yours?"

"I don't know. I'm just a soldier who's bad at his job."

"Maybe that's your power," she said. "Maybe you're supposed to protect the girls you find. Will you help us?"

I felt at home with her. Also, I wanted to see the taffy tree and play soccer.

"I think so."

"Good," Red said. "Then I will show you how to cross over into the other world. That's where people need protection most. And I'll show you how to do it without getting in trouble with your mother."

"How do you know so much about my mother?" I asked.

"She's my mother too," Red said. "In fact, she's the mother of everyone here. We're all hiding from her."

5

MY HEROIN-ADDICTED UNCLE
BECOMES MY BABYSITTER

My mother seemed happy with herself for choosing my step-father out of many suitors. He promised her a beautiful house by the Caspian Sea, which he bought and put in her name. She was pleased with her new summer beach villa and spent a lot of time furnishing it.

For the first several months of their marriage, we only vaca-tioned at our new beach house once a month and lived the rest of the time at Maman Bozorg's. Maman occupied the ground floor, and my mother, my stepfather, my baby sister Ava, and I—and, on weekends, my brother—occupied the two upper floors.

I had mixed feelings about living with my stepfather. On the one hand, I had to get used to a new person totally occupying my mother's attention, as my brother had before. On the other hand, my stepfather made my mother happy, and that, in turn, made me feel safe. She asked me to call him Baba. "From now on you will have a *real* father," she said. I already had a baba, but I did as she said anyway.

In those days, my main interactions with my mother took place in the morning. Even though she was now a housewife in a black chador, she followed the same routine she had when she worked at Revlon: get up early, spend an hour on makeup, and change outfits at least ten times before going to the bazaar to get spices, pickles, and meat. Her different outfits were now basically different kinds of headscarves, but I still thought she looked like a model and used to pretend I was her manager—though she never listened to my advice—and that her costume changes were for my approval. I told myself that I wanted to look like her when I grew up. She had long, silky black hair that smelled like wild roses. I felt proud when relatives assured me I had her looks. I used to lie on the bed across from her makeup table and watch her every movement.

"How do I look, Atash?" she'd ask, without glancing at me.

"Beautiful! That looks great, Mommy-joon."

She'd smile but was never satisfied. She'd go back to her dresser and take out another shade of eyeshadow. Eyeshadow and shoes were her main opportunities for color, since the rest of her was now covered in black, but she worked what she had—blue, brown, pink, black, and purple—harmonizing colors like a painter.

My mother smoked while she got ready, placing a lit cigarette in an ashtray beside the mirror in which she gazed upon herself. From across the room, I had a perfect vantage point from which to watch her reflection. I could adjust the angle of my seat so it would look as though she were looking at me too. She never smoked much of her cigarettes, letting them burn down almost totally in the ashtray. Sometimes she'd remember that she had put one there when there was only one drag left. Then she'd put it out, light another, take two puffs, and forget again as her reflection in the mirror took over. I sympathized with the discarded cigarettes.

"You shouldn't smoke," she would tell me sometimes as she finished applying purple tones to her eyes. "It's not a nice thing to do."

One thing I hated about living with my mother was having to play with the kid next door. I didn't like his games, but since my mother had started accompanying my stepfather to work—in order to make sure he was eating properly and not cheating on her—there was never anyone around I could complain to. My grandmother was hard of hearing and could hardly see anymore. She rarely left the kitchen. That meant I was alone in the rest of the house, so the kid next door used to come over, unannounced, to make sure I was okay. That usually meant insisting that he teach me things, grownup things—like, for example, French kissing, something he'd learned from magazines. Sometimes, on weekends when my brother was over, the kid next door would involve him in these games too. He would tell my brother to French-kiss me, and then, when we did, he'd make fun of us. "You two are disgusting! Brother and sister!" Then he'd laugh and make us do it again. Sometimes my brother sided with the kid next door to avoid being picked on himself.

I was afraid of telling on the kid next door because he was older and I was small and weak compared to him. He warned me not to talk about his games. Otherwise, he said, he'd hurt our grandmother. The few times I made an attempt to explain to my mother what was happening, she never really listened. Sometimes when the kid next door came over to play, I would go hide on the rooftop. Other times, I pretended our cat Maloos was missing and went out to look for her.

Maloos looked like a mini-leopard. She had big green eyes and would spend hours meticulously washing herself. Each spring, she would disappear for days to mate. Eventually, she'd appear on our doorstep, purring and pregnant. My mother would help her give birth by taking her to the roof, where we'd prepare a blanket for her. My mother would put on an apron and rub Maloos's belly, showing my brother and me how to calm the cat's nerves. Maloos's howls terrified us, but after half an hour, wet, slimy creatures would start to come out from between her legs, making small squeaking sounds. It was fascinating to see these furry balls rolling around with their eyes closed, while my mother picked up each and identified its gender.

One time, I thought Maloos had finished giving birth to a string of boys, but my mother announced that there was one last kitten. She was a girl, half the size of the others, and I noticed right away that Maloos ignored her. My mother noticed this too and seemed excited for what was about to happen. "This one is called 'The Runt,'" my mother explained. "She will become food for Maloos."

"I don't understand, Mommy-joon."

"In the cat world," my mother continued, "the mother eats the weakest kitten so she has energy to spend on the rest of her kittens."

I reached out to warm the shivering runt, but my mother yelled, "Atash! What are you doing? If the runt picks up your scent, Maloos won't eat her."

"Eat?" I still didn't understand.

"Yes, I've been explaining this for the past twenty minutes. It has to happen this way."

My brother seemed to understand better than I did. He said, "The weakest one. It's because she's the weakest."

I felt terror rush through me. I had to do something, fast. When my mother went out of the room to wash the blankets Maloos had soiled, I snatched the runt and ran as fast as I could down the three stories from our roof to the ground floor and out into the street. I rounded a corner and knocked on the door of our neighbor, an old lady who had always been kind to me.

"Ma'am, please," I panted. "Will you help me? Please, please, will you help?"

I showed her what I had in my hand. The runt didn't even cover the full span of my palm.

"My mother is going to feed her to her mother," I said. "It's because the strong ones feed on the weak ones so the strong ones have energy to live. But I don't want that. Will you make the runt strong too?"

The old lady had a sad look on her face. "Without her mother, she might not survive," the old lady said. But she took the runt, wrapped her in a towel, and brought her inside.

By the time I got back home, my mother had just reached the ground floor, breathless, thanks to her smoking habit. She knew right away what I'd done.

"Where's the runt?" she screamed.

"I lost her," I lied. "I dropped her and she ran away."

"Ran away? She couldn't even walk!"

"She did. And now she's gone."

My mother looked at me with contempt. "Six kittens and a mother might now die because of what you've done. There is a natural order of things, Atash. You can't change that."

One thing I loved about being at my mother's house was having my uncle Hossain come and stay with us. He used to pick me up in his arms and carry me on his back, but he always talked to me as though I were an adult. Uncle Hossain was very tall and had to bend down whenever he walked into any room, so I always felt as though I were sitting in the sky when I sat on his shoulders. People used to talk about how handsome he was. He had thick, full hair and a tall, athletic body. Everyone seemed to love Uncle Hossain, yet he seemed sad all the time. He smoked heroin a lot and used to get into heated arguments about it with his wife, who would lock him out of their house. This is why he'd often end up staying with us.

In Iran, smoking opium isn't taboo—my father and his friends frequently did it in front of their families, and their mothers often prepared it for them—but heroin is considered low class. Uncle Hossain's heroin habit was a source of shame to the entire family. Maman Bozorg always tried to defend him by blaming his addiction on the revolution. Hossain had been jailed for rebelling against the shah, and the guards had supposedly drugged him while he was in prison. "*Bezoor,*" she used to say. "By force." This explained to her why he was a full-blown addict by the time he was finally released.

When Hossain came to visit, he always stayed at least a few weeks. He became my babysitter—or maybe I was his. My grandmother asked me on several occasions to watch him and let her know if he used drugs in the house. I promised to tell her what I saw, but I never did.

Uncle Hossain was my protector. He always took my side when people were angry with me. He once said to my mother, "You don't treat Atash the way you treat your son. Atash deserves better." And of course, when Uncle Hossain was around, the kid next door didn't come over.

At nine, I knew everything about how to prepare heroin. This was a secret I shared with my uncle. I used to hide his drugs and the special spoon he used to mix them inside one of my dolls. My mother and grandmother always knew when Hossain was using, because of the sleepy look in his eyes, but they never found his stash. Once, they searched the entire house: every floor, every room, every closet. After a whole day of searching, they were beside themselves with frustration.

"Maybe he's just withdrawing and we're wrong," my mother said to Maman Bozorg.

"I know he's using," Maman Bozorg insisted. But there was no evidence.

Thanks to me and my doll, my uncle Hossain was never caught.

I was so proud of helping my uncle. Now, as someone who works with addicts, I cringe at my enabling, though I can't fault the little girl who wanted to protect the person who had always protected her. But in a way, I wish I hadn't been so clever. I wish I'd been caught.

One day, I was sitting alone with Uncle Hossain in the kitchen, wearing the red shirt he'd bought me three years before. It was way too small on me, but I wasn't ready to let it go.

"This is the shirt you got me as a gift," I reminded him. It took him a moment to process what I was saying. I saw he was already high. He brushed back my black hair and said, "Atash-joon, I will buy you a hundred new red shirts one day, when I get a job."

Hossain spread a little cloth over the floor near the kitchen stove so he could cook more heroin without burning the carpet. He knew Maman Bozorg protected her Shirazi rugs the way a mother bear guards her cubs. Then he asked, "Can you bring me your doll, Atash-joon?"

Following his instructions, I returned with his stash. He let me light the first drag of heroin. This was our ritual together. Then he smoked by himself, while I craned my neck to catch a whiff of the sweet-smelling smoke. Our cat Maloos came around as soon as the smoke began to spread in the air. After Hossain smoked for a bit, he began to nod, squirming, bending, and moving around like a cartoon. He mumbled words I couldn't understand. I sat next to him and watched with curiosity, petting Maloos. I played with his spoon and watched the door to make sure my grandmother wasn't coming back early.

After a few minutes, I looked up at the window and saw that the kid next door was walking into our yard. He was approaching our house. He must not have known my uncle was there.

"Uncle Hossain," I said, alarmed. "Please get up. The kid next door is here."

"Tell him to go away," he mumbled and fell back into his trance.

The kid next door came in. Apparently, the door had been left open. I remember that day he had a crazy look in his eyes. He put his index finger on his lips and walked toward me. I was speechless. I turned to my uncle again, but he was fully passed out.

The kid next door covered my mouth with his hand and dragged me upstairs toward the roof. I didn't understand what he wanted, so I didn't resist. When we got to the doorway of the roof, the kid looked to see if anyone was around. Then he shut the door behind us. He turned me around, held my mouth tight with one hand, and pulled up my skirt with the other. His hands smelled like earth, as if he'd been digging in the dirt. He dragged me over to a pile of clothes Maman Bozorg had stored on the far side of the roof, and pushed me over it. I felt that strange sensation in my belly again and felt as though my back were breaking. I opened my mouth, waiting for a birdsong to come, but nothing came. The kid made angry noises; I didn't know what they meant. My eyes searched the rooftops for someone who might be watching. But all the rooftop doors were closed.

The pain got more intense. The kid started making louder sounds. Uglier sounds. My vision was blurred, but I couldn't rub my eyes because my hands were pinned beneath my chest. I felt the wind pick up and things start to blow around. I could dimly make out a crack in the door to our roof. Then the crack widened. *Maybe it's my uncle,* I thought, but the door just closed again, trembling with the movements of the wind. There was nothing there, but there was something moving anyway. *There's something inside me,* I thought. *How can there be something inside me?*

There are miles and miles of land inside you. No matter how much others think they're inside, they never reach you. There is always further to hide.

Suddenly, I thought I saw a pair of eyes in the crack of the door. They were light and beautiful and lined with dark eyeliner. Then there was a mouth, wide open, staring horrified back at me. *Mommy? Mommy!* I called out and tried to reach for the face in the crack of the door.

But it vanished. I looked again and saw nothing but trembling blackness swinging back and forth. The kid's voice got quieter. Then I heard him pull up his pants. He said, "If you tell anyone you'll be in big trouble." I felt him pull away from me, and in a few moments, I found enough courage to tilt my head slightly, just in time to see him jumping over the railing that separated our roof from his. Then he was gone.

I pulled up my underwear and sat on the last step of the staircase. I cried for a while, thinking over what he'd said.

"If you tell anyone you'll be in big trouble."

Then I remembered my uncle.

He's still downstairs! How could you forget him?

I started to move toward the steps, but it was at that moment that I realized I couldn't walk. My legs were shaking and I was hobbling like Maman Bozorg. I realized there was blood on my legs, underwear, and shirt. My favorite shirt. What was I going to tell Uncle Hossain?

After a while, I made it downstairs. My uncle was lying on the floor. *He's dead*, I thought.

"Uncle Hossain, get up!" I screamed. I held him, kissing his forehead and begging to open his eyes, but he didn't. I pleaded with God. I said, "God, if you let my uncle live, I won't tell anyone about the kid next door. Or the man in Qom." But there was no movement. *I've killed my uncle*, I thought.

I'm not sure why, but at that moment I remembered a movie called *Atash-bedoone dood—Fire Without Smoke*—that I'd seen a few days before. In the film, a raging fire killed a house full of people and carried them to heaven, where there were rivers and trees and kids playing without worrying about food or ever being hurt.

It's okay to want to die. Uncle Hossain is dead. Many good people are dead. They're all waiting on the other side.

I found the matches my uncle had been using to cook heroin and went to my mother's walk-in closet, the one I used to play hide-and-seek with my brother in. There were so many clothes stashed there that it was easy to get lost. I sat down in the middle of the closet and stared at the darkness.

I'm here with you.

I lit a first match and threw it over toward the right corner of the closet. I imagined myself evaporating, like a raindrop in the sun. But the match went out in the air. I lit another and threw it at the space near my right foot. It caught on one of my mother's blouses. I picked up the blouse and threw it over to the other corner of the closet. Then I lit a third match and threw it behind me. The fire started to get bigger. Before I knew it, I was roasting. There was smoke everywhere and I couldn't breathe. The smell of my own burning hair was making me sick.

This was a mistake.
Get help.
Scream.

"Atash! Atash! Atash!" I screamed. "Fire! Fire! Fire!" It felt strange to scream my own name at the top of my lungs.

Just then, Uncle Hossain's big hands appeared out of nowhere. I could hardly see him because of the smoke, but I knew his hands. The hands passed through the fire, lifted me into the air, and pulled me out of the closet. In the light of the room, I saw that Hossain's shirt had also caught fire. He put out the flames coming from his chest while he grabbed a nearby blanket and wrapped me in it. He looked like a madman in battle, as though he were fighting a dragon.

When he'd finally put out the fire, he looked at his burnt hands and began to blow on them. He had tears in his eyes. I was still wrapped in the blanket. He picked me up and checked my skin for injuries. There were black holes in my shirt, but no real burns. I thought he was going to yell at me. Instead, he kissed me over and over and thanked God I was alive.

"I thought you were dead on the floor," I said.

"Please forgive me," he cried. I didn't understand why he was pleading for my forgiveness. I thought I was the one who had to be forgiven. Uncle Hossain kept crying and his cries got louder and louder. But I was so exhausted that his cries seemed like a lullaby to me. Gradually, they put me to sleep.

When I woke in the middle of the night I heard my mother, stepfather, and grandmother yelling at my uncle in the kitchen. I couldn't see them because I was still on the couch in the living room. I pretended to be asleep, but I heard every word.

"I swear I'll stop using," Uncle Hossain said. He told them that, this time, things would be different. "This is the end of the line," I heard him say to Maman Bozorg. "Seeing Atash in the middle of that fire was the end of the line for me." Then a silence fell on the house.

The next day, I wondered about the voice I had heard inside me. It seemed to want me to destroy things, but then again, it also helped me. It would be years before I understood that voice as a part of myself talking to me. For the moment, it just scared me.

Uncle Hossain was telling the truth; he sobered up after all. But this was a difficult process for him, as it was for everyone else in the house, especially me. He had us lock him in the basement for two weeks. By day two, I could hear him yelling and screaming all the way from the top floor of our house. "I'm fine now! Hey, Maman! Let me go! I'm better!"

He sounded like a wounded beast. But my grandmother was stubborn and wouldn't let him out till two weeks had passed. She assured me that he really was okay and that his time in the basement was just a part of his journey toward getting better, but it was hard to hear him scream. My grandmother cried for him too, but she wouldn't relent. She cooked him lavish stews, dishes of rice, and kettles of tea, and slid them through the small window in the door that led to the basement. This was the only safe way to deliver him meals. We were all scared of opening the window, for fear Hossain would come jumping through it like a loose beast. Maman Bozorg promised me that, when Hossain was cured, I would be the one to unlock the door for him.

It seemed strange to me that a little bit of smoke could have such an effect on such a big man and that someone who seemed invincible to me would need so much help from us. It was only when I tried to quit drinking myself, years later, that I felt that same howling in me and realized there was no way I could face that experience alone.

I counted the days and minutes till I could free my uncle. Every night, when I tried to sleep, I heard his crying. When I finally did fall asleep, I dreamed of a fire no one could put out, whose high flames burned our house and killed my mother and Maman Bozorg. In my dreams, I was responsible for their deaths. For some reason, this thought made me want to pee. In the dream, I peed behind a tree and felt relieved. But when I peed in my dream, I also peed in my real bed.

I used to wake up frightened by the strange mixture of pleasure and shame in peeing my bed. My mother and Maman Bozorg were disturbed by my regressive behavior. "What could be wrong with her?" they asked. Their concern made me happy, though I knew I'd never tell them why. They came up with a new rule for me, which was to escort me to the bathroom every night before bed to make sure I peed. This had little effect. Then my mother bought me a new mattress and said, "With this mattress, we can start fresh again." She must have bought several before realizing I was not going to stop wetting the bed. Then there came a day when she told me there would be no new mattresses, and that if I peed again, I'd have to sleep in my urine. So I learned not to mind sleeping in my own pee.

Eventually, my mother couldn't take the smell and threw out my mattress. I was then demoted from pants to diapers, which made me feel even more ashamed. Gradually, my friends from the House of Stone would wake me up in the middle of a dream to remind me to go to the bathroom. It was only because of them that I stopped wetting my bed. Once my peeing problem subsided, however, I started washing my hands obsessively again.

As a therapist now, I'm familiar with these types of obsessive-compulsive patterns. But what really strikes me, as I look back, is how much creativity I had in dealing with my problems. The House of Stone was a great resource, and I'm amazed at how brilliantly my younger self accessed it.

Finally, the day came when we were to let Uncle Hossain out of the basement. We gathered in the courtyard, by the big, broad door that led to the basement. Maman Bozorg, my mother, and my brother watched as I snatched the key and unlocked the door, and Uncle Hossain came staggering out into the sunlight, his eyes stuck shut, like an animal's after hibernation. His beard was huge and his hands still had scabs on them, but he was smiling. *He looks like a lion*, I thought.

After Hossain quit using heroin, no one ever talked about the fire or my peeing problem again. It was as though they wanted to forget. I certainly wanted to forget that day with the matches in the closet too. Also, my experience with the kid next door, though the abuse continued for many years.

My uncle would always say he owed his sobriety to me. And I owed my life to him too, but I never told him that. I think he knew. I was sad when his wife finally came to our house to take him home. She kissed me and said I was his guardian angel, but she didn't want to stay too long. Shortly after arriving, she had his bags in her hand and was at the door. As she was leaving, she turned to Maman Bozorg and said, "Thank you." But Maman Bozorg just looked away. We all knew that Maman did not like Hossain's wife and blamed her for her son's sadness. My uncle kissed me goodbye and promised to visit. He kept his promise and came to see me every Friday, though he didn't stay over. He looked better each time I saw him and called me his *khoosh-qadam*, his "lucky charm."

The kid next door stopped his visits for a while after he heard about the fire. I was happy not to see him in real life, but he still visited me in my dreams. Sometimes he and the hanged man came together to hunt for me. I ran from them in terror as they ran after me. The faster I ran, the closer they got. But I always woke before they caught me.

Like the runt, I knew I could survive. For months, I watched as the old lady on my block fed the runt saucers of cow's milk. I hoped that the runt would grow to be as big as a cow. I also visited Maloos on the roof every day and asked her for forgiveness. "I know those are the rules, Maloos-joon," I said, "But sometimes we have to change them." Maloos yawned in approval.

The old lady and I became friends. Each day, I would visit her and she'd tell me that her own kids and grandkids didn't come over as much as I did. She fed me sweet zulbia while I built the runt a house out of cardboard, newspaper, and cotton balls. The runt grew more slowly than Maloos's other kittens, but little by little, the runt's voice changed from small squeaks to big meows. After a few months, the old lady let the runt play with me in her garden. Soon after, the runt was roaming the neighborhood, as other cats did.

One day, the runt ran into our garden and into the path of her mother Maloos. Maloos's fur stood on end and she looked as though she'd seen a ghost. But the runt just turned and went to the other side of the garden. She was now even bigger than her mother.

"Wow, look at this beautiful new cat who showed up," my mother and brother said. Their cluelessness made me giggle.

I learned that day that creatures can be small and defeated but still grow up to find their own power. To this day, I think of the runt as my first teacher.

6

ORANGE

I'm Orange. I'm the oldest of the girls who live in the House of Stone. I take care of the others and try to give them wisdom when I can. Sometimes I get lonely, though. The House is dark and damp, and often I feel the walls are too tight for my body. The narrow corridors and rooms feel like sleeves on a dress that fit too tightly.

I don't remember when I started exploring the upper levels of the House, but at some point, I discovered a skylight that lets light in, and beyond it, a secret staircase that leads to a small ledge just wide enough for one person to sit on. I began spending time up there, away from the little ones, bathing in the sun. From there, I could also make sure no one was approaching the House. Especially the Witch.

If I had a religion, it would revolve around the sun. The sun makes flowers and trees bloom and takes away every bad smell. I decided to build a shrine to the sun up on the ledge. I took all the broken mirrors I found in the House and strung them in a circle on the ledge, so that, at any time of day, the sun's brilliance would be magnified. I'd sit for hours at the center of my sun-circle, till my skin turned the color of clay by the sea.

I'd come down for dinner glowing, and all the kids would tell me how magnificent my skin looked. When I hugged them, they felt warm for hours.

One day, I fell asleep sunbathing on my ledge and dreamed a horrible dream. I was walking through a library full of books that told the stories of all our memories. I was thinking in the dream how important it is to keep a library like that safe, when I kicked over a lamp and the books started to burn. I woke up screaming and realized I, too, was in pain: I'd been sleeping in the sun, and my skin was severely burned. I ran my hands over my arms to soothe them, but the skin started to flake off, like dried clay. I panicked and ran downstairs. The others screamed when they saw me.

"Where have you been?" Blue said. "It's been two days."

I had no idea what time it was. "Everything hurts," I said.

The kids brought me oils and creams and gels and aloe, but nothing helped. The pain was so bad that I started to lose consciousness, and as I did, I heard Red's little voice from the top of the stairs.

"Mirrors!" she cried. "There's light everywhere! You can see where the House of Stone is from across the forest! Now the Witch will know where we are!"

I lost consciousness completely.

7

HEAVEN ON EARTH

My mother seemed sadder every day. Unemployed and mostly alone with a new baby, she cried most of the day. But during this time, a new dynamic between me and her began to emerge. Perched in front of her new housewife's stove, she'd listen to me bring her gossip from the outside world. She particularly liked it when I told her news about my father, whom she'd shifted from being angry at to missing.

"I should've stayed with your Baba," she'd say to me. "Tell me, what's his wife like?"

I sensed an opportunity to get closer to her and recited long stories about my father. Sometimes, I exaggerated. Once, I said that my father had come to my parent-teacher conference and that all the teachers at my school had fallen in love with him at first sight. I knew how to inflame her jealousy and thereby hold her attention.

"How do you know that?" she said, eyes widening. "You're just a kid."

"Well," I said, aware of my new power, "since his visit, my teachers have been giving me the highest grades. And when they give me back my homework assignments, they say, 'Be sure to send my regards to Mr. Yaghmaian.' Of course, I don't tell him that," I assured her.

Storytelling has always been a form of protection for me. For years, when I used to tell people about this period in my life—from age ten to eleven—I would tell them how beautiful the Caspian Sea was, or how gorgeous the rolling mountains near our beachfront property were. Even when I first sat down to write this book, I was tempted to focus on those picturesque scenes. But then I'd feel a sickness in my belly, which eventually said to me: Those were the worst days of my life. Those were days when I became isolated, when people hit me and degraded me, when I saw how no one intervened or objected. And I had to rethink my habit of storytelling, because was I really protecting myself by remembering only the beauty?

In one more reversal, my father decided again to give up full custody of my brother to my mother. His new wife was expecting, and his own relatives were pressuring him to focus on his new family. My mother chose to interpret this surrender as a sign of his eternal passion for her, and she told my stepfather exactly that. "You see how he still cares for me?" My stepfather arched an eyebrow and said, "He's just trying to get rid of an extra kid."

My stepfather never got angry at my mother when she tried to make him jealous. Instead, he just took away her freedom, little by little. First, he asked her not to go shopping any more.

"I have a reputation here," he said. "What will people think of a woman who has to go into disgusting stores alone?"

Then, a few days later, at dinner, he launched into a speech about how Tehran was too overpopulated and how much more preferable the suburbs were.

"I've decided that we're going to leave Tehran," he said.

My mother and I looked at each other. Where were we going to go? But we said nothing. We looked down and continued eating our dinner as if he hadn't said anything.

People call Ramsar *Behisht-e zamin,* or "Heaven on Earth." It's a green town with a pleasant climate located in the area north of Tehran called Shomal (literally, North) along the Caspian Sea. Ramsar is where many rich people from Tehran take their summer vacations, but the locals live much simpler, poorer lives.

When we were still vacationers, it would take us seven hours to drive from Tehran to Ramsar, but the drive was fun because my brother and my sister and I would get lost in the anticipation of getting to play with hundreds of other kids on summer break. My little sister Ava would sleep in the back seat of our car, on my left, while my brother, seated at the window on my right, would wave to children in the other cars along the highway. Whenever adults noticed us, we'd stick our tongues out at them and then, giggling, crumple down into our seats to hide.

One time, when our car was stuck in traffic, still in the outskirts of Tehran, I looked out the window and saw a woman walking alongside our car. She had on a green robe and held a basket of wild roses. She was very beautiful.

Suddenly my mother called out, "Kids, look! A mirage."

I turned to face the front. Ahead, the road was filled with dips that seemed to be full of water, but as we got closer, the water evaporated.

"Mommy-joon," I asked, "can people be mirages too?"

She laughed. "Only if you're crazy, sweetie."

Those were the days when I used to see people walking next to me all the time, people I knew my family members couldn't see. *Maybe they're evaporating people,* I thought.

I no longer see people that others don't. I experience these characters now only as parts of myself. But what a gift those childhood visions were! For if I had known then that they were just my own inner parts, I would never have found protection or comfort in them. How is it that children have so much wisdom?

As the city got further behind us, I would watch the farms bleed into one other, until the stretch of roads that ducked between large mountains and linked all the northern towns seemed to be one continuous pasture. Unlike Tehran, whose topography is mostly naked rock, the northern mountains are lush and dressed with thousands of green trees. I would be absorbed in how the roads curved like snakes and wove in and out of the bellies of the hills. As we passed one particular tunnel through a mountain, I always knew that we were halfway to the sea.

At the midpoint of our journey, where the climate abruptly changes from arid to humid, my stepfather would stop on the road to rest at his favorite teahouse. My brother and I would get out of the car and laugh at how our clothes stuck to our bodies and my hair curled up. My mother would explain, as though she hadn't the summer before, that this was a phenomenon that had to do with humidity. Even her own hair, which looked straight in Tehran, curled up in Ramsar.

I loved the beach at Ramsar. In those days, just after the revolution, the sand was pristine and everyone was happy—especially my mother, who got to wear tighter and more revealing clothing. The Islamic Republic had already banned women from wearing bathing suits, but the rules were not as strict as they would become in the following years, when men and women were separated by curtains on the beach. At age nine, I was still allowed to wear the bikini my mother bought for me. It was too big for my scrawny nine-year-old body, and I fantasized about losing the top so I could look more like my brother, whom everyone loved and let do as he pleased. The next year, though, I would lose even the right to wear any kind of bathing suit.

I particularly loved eating caviar at the beach. When I came to America, I was shocked to learn that caviar is something only rich people eat. But the Caspian Sea is home to the beluga sturgeon, whose roe makes the finest caviar in the world, and it was so abundant in those days that we ate it on toast for breakfast. Caviar is technically forbidden (*haram*) in Islam, though Khomeini famously and cynically declared it lawful (*halal*) in 1983. But in our tiny town on the sea, very little of that religious controversy had reached us yet. So we continued to pop those magical little sea-bubbles of saltiness in our mouths all summer.

It was the summer of 1981 when I came home from playing outside and saw my mother and stepfather fighting in the kitchen. My stepfather kept saying, "We have no other choice."

"Who's going to take care of Maman Bozorg if we stay here?" my mother asked.

"She can visit as much as she wants, but this is going to be our permanent home." He said this definitively. But my mother continued to question him.

"But why here?" She started to cry.

"We're in the middle of a war," he said.

"The bombing of Tehran is over. Both sides are in a stalemate now. There's only a little fighting in the south."

"Well *I* feel safer here," he repeated. "You're very naive. This is going to be a long war. It's better to be among good country people, among beautiful rice farms."

"You mean living among ghosts? Among houses that are so far apart? Among people who never open their mouths except to sell something to a tourist? And what will you do for work here? Did you think of that? Thank God we have savings, but how long will that money last?"

My stepfather didn't answer. He looked pale, all of a sudden, like a man who had just witnessed his own death.

"Are you listening?" My mother's voice started to rise. "We must have no more than . . . no more than . . . " My mother's voice trailed off. It was clear she had no real idea about his finances.

Then my stepfather said, "It was a month ago. The trucks carrying my clothing stock were hit by missiles. What other choice do we have but to stay here?"

A smile crossed my mother's face, as though my stepfather had told a joke.

"What are you saying?" she said.

"Ashes," he said. "Everything. Even the factory is gone. All of it."

The smile on my mother's face spread into a giggle, then faded into a low mumbling sound. Her face was yellow and contorted. I instinctively ran to get her a tissue. When I returned, she was sitting on the living room floor. I heard my stepfather ask her to take off her gold bracelets.

"I'm sorry," he said. "I'll buy you more soon."

She folded her arms, so the bracelets, which completely covered her forearms, were hidden. She looked like a child holding her doll back from a bully.

My stepfather sat back in his chair and rubbed his sweaty hands together. He and my mother sat facing each other for hours. They smoked cigarettes in silence and stared at the air. At the end of the night, though, my mother took off her bracelets one by one and handed them over to him.

"I'll never forgive you," she said.

"There is one truck with some clothes left," he said. "I'll sell those first, I promise."

He never sold that shipment, though. Those clothes were stacked in one of our bedrooms for a long time. My stepfather told my mother that he was looking for a loan to open a boutique with.

"Once I open that store," he said, "I will sell those clothes and buy you new bracelets with the money."

I didn't get to say goodbye to my father, my friends, Siavash, or my teachers. There was no farewell; we just stayed on in our summer home long after everyone else had returned to the city in the fall. I was sad to leave everything I knew and scared to start over in fifth grade with new friends, new teachers, and a new home.

For years, I did everything I could to avoid goodbyes. Being present to separation or loss always seemed to me like it made things worse. It was only later, in social-work school, when I learned about proper termination of therapy with a client, that I realized I'd been missing out on the healing power of goodbyes. Goodbyes hurt, yes, but never getting to acknowledge how much a person or place means to you hurts even more.

I reassured myself that, in the backyard of our new house, I had a huge garden, one in which I could plant tomatoes, basil, potatoes, watermelon, and lettuce. We already had a few apple, orange, and mulberry trees that I'd started to groom. Within a few days, I cleared a plot of soil and started to bring the garden back to life. Since it was already autumn, I asked a neighbor to help me choose the plants that would make it through the winter. He suggested witch hazel and *kulus* (coleus).

I had no winter clothes: all my things were back in Tehran, and I was still mainly wearing my brother's hand-me-downs. My stepfather once took my brother and me on a guilt-induced shopping trip to some local stores, but the winter coats there were hideous. The mood around me got colder as the air did.

In September, my stepfather registered my brother at an all-boys school, for sixth grade. My mother registered me at one of the nearby all-girls schools, for fifth grade. This particular school was right on the water, and I often heard the waves from my classroom. I began to fall in love with the Caspian Sea, and I taught myself to forget about my friends in Tehran by imagining that the ocean was my new best friend. My stepfather was right about one thing: there were no Iraqi planes flying over Ramsar, dropping explosives. I no longer heard sirens. There were no underground bomb shelters.

My fifth-grade teacher was Mrs. Rushanas. She was a tall, big-boned lady, with a round, yellow face that reminded me of one of those delicious Lebanon apples you can find in almost any store in Iran. I wanted to like her. All my teachers in Tehran had been so loving; I was sure she would be the same.

My illusions were shattered the first week, however, when she asked the students in our class to share an event that had made a difference in our lives. All my classmates told stories about the day their younger siblings were born, the first day they'd gone to school, or when their fathers had bought them their first farm animals. Everyone giggled at every story. When my turn came to stand in front of the class, everyone was quiet. They wanted to hear what the stranger from the big city was going to say.

I told them the story of the night when I was deep in sleep and my father came into the room to wake me up, yelling, "We have to evacuate the house!" I told the class about the sound of warplanes and how they got louder as they got closer, as though they were right above our building. I told them about how our neighbors were crying and running down the stairs as the deafening sounds of bombs shook our building and shattered our windows. I told them about the dead people I saw and art projects I made from bullet shells. "There was a man they hanged . . . "

"That will do!" Mrs. Rushanas yelled. She dismissed class early and told me to speak with her after. As they exited, my classmates looked at me as though I were a beast. "You're going to get it," one of the girls said and walked away.

Mrs. Rushanas walked her large frame toward one of the desk drawers and got out a big wooden stick. She raised it in the air and brought it down so hard on my desk that it broke in half.

"I don't feel sorry for privileged Tehrani people," she said to no one in particular. Then she bent down to pick up the other half of her broken wooden stick.

"I'm sorry," I said. "I didn't mean to do any harm." Her face was turning the color of a pomegranate.

"*Saket bash,*" she hissed. "Be quiet." Then she made a sound that reminded me of a cow being bitten by a horsefly. "Next time I'm going to break this stick over your head," she said. "Now leave."

I left with my head down. The other girls told me that Mrs. Rushanas was the head teacher in school. Everyone was terrified of her—including the other teachers—and before lunch was over I had learned the importance of not being seen by her.

When I work with students these days, I see right away which ones have already mastered the art of being invisible. The ones whose names teachers still don't know by November. The ones who turn in just enough work not to be called out. These are the first students I talk to in private, because I understand the art of invisibility, where it comes from—and because I want to know how these kids learned it for themselves. And yet, there are always one or two I miss. Graduation comes, and I realize, all of a sudden, that their ability to be invisible was better than I anticipated.

At recess on my first day, all the students met up outside. I had no one to meet, so I imagined that the sea was waiting for me. When I got to the shore, I took off my shoes and walked barefoot on the sand. It seemed clear to me that I had made a mistake talking about myself.

You don't have to share yourself with anyone. You don't have to show anyone your tears. You have us. In the quiet by the sea, you can hear all of us with you. Listen for that.

In the days that followed, I tried to befriend other kids, but they stayed away, calling me *Divooneh Tehrani*, "the crazy girl from Tehran." I got used to sitting by myself under the huge trees that stood at the edge of the schoolyard. Their branches sheltered me as I read books in their shade. I learned about Iranian history, about Cyrus and Darius the Great.

"Put your books away," Mrs. Rushanas told us in class one day. "You are going to be tested orally today, a week earlier than we originally planned." Her voice brought me back from a daydream. The girls made dissatisfied sounds.

"Shhhhhh," Mrs. Rushanas said. "Now, when I call your name, rise and come up to the front." "Yaghmaian," "Yazdian," "Hossaini," "Haydari." She liked calling us by our last names.

She asked the four of us to read a few passages from a book. Some of it was poetry, some prose. We did what she asked. It wasn't good enough. We did it again. Then she asked us a few questions about history and geography. We didn't remember the right answers.

"Haydari and Yaghmaian, you two stand by the board and face the class. Put your arms up in the air."

We did this.

"Higher!" she ordered. "Like a captured soldier begging for mercy." We waited for her to approach, but she didn't. Apparently, she just wanted us to keep standing there like that for the rest of the class period. Then she turned her attention to the other two girls. She made them hold out their hands, palms facing up, and brought her new wooden stick down with a smack on their tender skin.

"Let this be a lesson for all of you," she said to the class. "Always be ready for a test."

There were tears streaming down the girls' cheeks, but they were allowed to return to their seats. Haydari and I still awaited further instruction as Mrs. Rushanas kept on teaching. We were stranded at the front of the class. As the minutes passed, our arms started to drift down. It was at this point that Mrs. Rushanas noticed us.

"Get your arms back up!" she yelled. As the blood drained from my arms, my body started to feel lighter. Pretty soon, I couldn't hear what Mrs. Rushanas was saying anymore. I felt graceful, standing there, like some noble princess whose royal identity hadn't yet been discovered. I imagined Mrs. Rushanas begging for mercy when she realized whom it was that she had been treating so disrespectfully.

The Witch has no power over you, princess! Look at your hands. They are covered in ivy. Nothing can get to them now, not even the sharpest sword in the world. You are new again, with new skin.

"It's over," I heard a voice say.

It was Haydari, still standing next to me. I looked at her closely for the first time. She was shorter than I was, wearing heels and designer jeans under her long tunic. I never saw anyone our age wearing heels before.

"It's time to go home," she said. I looked around; the whole class was gone. There was only Haydari and I—and, I noticed, another girl standing with us, who was only half our height. Haydari stepped toward me.

"You can call me by my first name," she said. "I'm Batool."

I smiled, but I didn't say anything. The small girl followed suit. "I'm Zahra," she said in a mouse-like voice. "Are you okay?"

"Yes, why?"

"You looked like a statue."

"Like a dead person standing up," Batool added. "You didn't move or cry the whole time. Even when she made you stand on one foot and poured all that chalk dust on you."

"Chalk dust?"

I looked down at my navy blue uniform. It was totally white. Then I realized how sore my arms and right leg were. I was totally confused and tried to change the subject.

"Are you the same age as we are?" I asked Zahra. "Why are you so little?"

"I was born like this," she replied. "My mother says I won't grow more, but I'm also eleven, just like you."

"Why can't you grow? Are you sick?"

"Not sick, but I can't play like the other kids. I get tired really quickly. The doctors don't know why."

"Does Mrs. Rushanas make fun of everybody like this?"

"Everybody," Zahra said severely. "When I get a question wrong, the teacher puts me in the trashcan." She pointed to the basket by the teacher's desk. "She does it because I fit in there so perfectly, and it makes the class laugh."

I didn't know what to say to this.

"Let's go. We're going to miss the bus," Batool said.

"I'm so sorry," I said to Zahra. "Have you told your father or the dean?"

"Everyone's afraid of her," Zahra said. "One girl brought in her father to confront Mrs. Rushanas. They met together for a while in private—I don't know what happened—but when they came out, they dragged the girl into the prayer room and beat her together. After that, no one dared bring in their parents again."

In the bus, we sat in silence, defeated by the day. I yearned for Tehran, my teachers and their soft manners, and a world where things made sense: a world without chalk dust, standing on one leg, or cruelty. When I got home, I found my mother also distraught, crying and complaining about her unfortunate life. She and my stepfather had been yelling again. She was mad at him for not working and failing to bring home groceries.

"I can't give my kids mashed potatoes for dinner!" She was hissing, like a cat defending her territory. My stepfather was quiet as always, but I knew his style was to sit back and let an argument escalate, like someone watching a fire start to catch. My mother began to talk to herself, about how she missed my father, about how my stepfather had taken her away from her one true love.

"No one loves me," she concluded, as she usually did during one of her scenes.

And I replied, as always, "I do, Mommy-joon."

"You don't even know what love is," she said.

"Yes, I do. Love is when I stay up all night and pray till dawn that nothing bad happens to you." This usually worked with her. I had many of these one-liners in the bank. For instance, I told her once that in theater class, the teacher had asked us to do a crying scene, and no one could do it but me, because I had been thinking about what life would be like if she were dead. She liked that a lot.

My mother got up from where she was sitting and took my hand.

"It's time to dance and be happy now," she announced, putting a tape of the famous Iranian singer Hayideh on the stereo. "Delamo Shekastee" (You Broke My Heart) started to play, and as the rhythmic pulse grew, my mother started to dance.

"Kids!" she exclaimed. "Get up and join Mommy."

I wasn't sure I wanted to dance, but before I knew it, we were all jumping up and down. My stepfather got up and went to his room, holding little Ava's hand in his. My mother shouted after him, "You can't keep me miserable forever! I have my kids!"

But my stepfather got his revenge in the end. A week later, he declared that she wasn't allowed to do any shopping anymore or talk to anyone in the street. My mother, as always, obeyed him but made sure to make a pass at any man who came over.

I was always impressed by my mother's powers of seduction, and for a long time, I wanted to be just like her. But as my life got bigger, I realized what a thin sliver of life her brand of sexuality was. And I saw that what my mother was trying to do by being sexy wasn't actually self-expression or self-respect but a desperate attempt to get something very small: a loaf of bread or a moment of revenge.

One time, a banker came to the house. He apparently had the power to approve or deny a loan for us, which we desperately needed. He stared at my mother the whole time. At one point, she got up, went to her bedroom, put on a skin-tight purple dress beneath her chador, and came back also wearing copious amounts of red lipstick and perfume. She brought a tray of tea into the living room and sat facing the banker. When he had drunk the tea, she placed the hem of her chador between her lips and tongue and stood up provocatively. Then, she sauntered over to the kitchen, letting the fabric slip off her head to the floor, revealing her long, flowing hair and supple body beneath the tight dress. When she reached the kitchen, she yelled, "Atash! My God! My chador must have fallen off. Can you get it for me?"

"Yes, Mommy," I said, running after her, the black fabric trailing from my hand like a kite.

I think you could actually see the smoke coming out of my stepfather's ears. But it didn't matter. He got the loan because of what she'd done and also because she came into the room one more time and asked the banker flatly, "Are you going to give it to us or not?"

"Absolutely," he said, looking my mother up and down.

That night, my stepfather started to berate my mother for her behavior, but she just scoffed and said that if our finances had been left up to his *orzeh*—his competence—we would have gone another night without dinner.

It wasn't just our family who became poor. In those wartime years, there was no way to get basic necessities in a town like Ramsar, even if a person had money. The supermarkets were nearly empty, apart from a few canned goods. Some of the richer people bought meat on the black market for exorbitant prices. We certainly didn't have that kind of wealth, but somehow my mother managed to get us meat a few times a week. I don't know whether she did so with her looks, or her personality, but we all knew it wasn't with money.

There was a period of a few months, however, when there was absolutely no fresh food. The government cut supplies to the point where people were being turned away from the ration lines. This was happening to everyone, but as was always the case with my mother, she told us to keep our lack of food a secret from my classmates and neighbors. Sometimes, she would make us sit down and imagine we were eating a fancy meal. She'd put on music, dance around the table, and name different dishes of the imaginary stews and meats we were invited to take bites of. This was always my favorite game.

Some of our neighbors were helpful at this time. They had heard about my stepfather's loss of business and offered him and my mother odd jobs, but neither ever took them up on any of these offers.

"Who do these peasants think they are, offering us jobs?" my stepfather would say.

"They just want to help," my mother would counter. "We shouldn't be ungrateful. I'm not going to turn them away."

"They want to help you because you are beautiful," he'd complain. "They want to make sure that I fail even more, so that they can have you for themselves."

Our neighbors eventually caught on to my stepfather's condescension and stopped offering. My mother went to greater and greater lengths to make dinner out of anything she could. While cooking basmati rice and pomegranate stew, she would talk to herself and say things like, "I knew I should never have married again. He's nothing but bad luck."

Every time she said "bad luck," I felt my intestines wriggle. I knew it was only a matter of time till I ended up with the blame for her circumstances.

8

GREEN

I'm Green. I watch over the gardens that surround the House of Stone. People call me the Medicine Woman, because I know the properties of every plant in the forest, and I know how to use these plants to make teas that can cure whatever ails a person. I'm a good cook too. Even though people in the House of Stone don't actually get hungry, they appreciate my cooking. It brings us together.

I talk to plants and they talk to me too. From them, I learn all sorts of secrets about the Witch, where she goes and what she does, and about the health of the forest. From the plants, I learn about the sadness of those who come here. The plants told me how Red flew here as a bird, how Blue was pulled through a wall, how Orange arrived as a spark of fire. I feel their pain as though it were mine. I'm determined to help them heal.

I have this ability: whatever I touch turns to vegetation. My gift can both heal and hurt, which is why I wear white gloves all the time.

Once, Orange set herself on fire with mirrors. Her skin burned off completely and she needed new skin. I wandered the forest for days gathering leaves the exact color of her old skin, mixing them with ochre dirt, and sewing the whole thing together with a needle and thread. Then I took off my gloves and lay my bare hands on the new skin. It came to life, and we were able to cover Orange with it.

Red was very upset that Orange's mirrors might have given away the location of our House, so I volunteered to conceal the mountain even more. I climbed the whole height of the mountain, and as I lay my hands over its rocks, ivy grew and grew upon it, till it was covered with a jungle so thick that not even the most courageous explorer would approach it.

When I finished my work, however, I realized someone had been watching me the whole time. This curious person walked like a girl, though she looked a lot like a man. She was wearing riding boots; her arms were muscular and well-defined. Above her top lip, thick hair sprouted. She kept her head covered with a sort of turban.

I asked her what her name was, but she just smiled. I realized after a while that she wasn't going to use words, so I stuck to yes-or-no questions. Was she looking for someone? She nodded again and pointed to a cluster of wild roses nearby.

"Scarlet?" I asked.

She blinked.

"Okay," I said. "But you can't stay here. You can't stand in front of our mountain. Someone might see."

She remained expressionless and stood her ground.

I decided to leave her. I took the long way back to our House so she wouldn't see the entrance. At dinner, I asked Scarlet about the girl in riding boots.

"The mute stable girl? She's a friend of mine. Isn't she handsome?"

I told Scarlet that isn't the point. The girl could give away our location.

"I'm not like you," Scarlet said. "I need to be around different people. I'm dying of loneliness in this stupid House."

The next day, the mute stable girl was still standing in front of our mountain. This time, however, she was seated on top of a mangy, spotted horse.

"Listen," I said. "You seem very nice and Scarlet likes you, but you have to go."

The stable girl turned her horse around so her back was facing me. It takes a lot to get me upset, but I could feel myself getting frustrated.

I reached out for one of her stirrups and realized—too late— that my gloves were off. As soon as my hand made contact with the stable girl's foot, her leg began to flower into a bouquet of roses. They climbed her torso, arms, and head, till she was nothing but flowers. The flowers continued to grow, cascading over the saddle and onto the ground. The mangy horse, frightened, galloped off.

I was horrified by what I'd done, but I was determined to find a solution without telling Scarlet. I gathered the roses and planted them behind the House till I could figure out how to turn them back into the stable girl. Within a few days, they grew into an enormous bush. All the girls marveled at it and liked to sit in its shade, but none knew the truth about what had happened.

9

WORDS AND RIVERS

In sixth grade, I developed a new problem. I started to notice that I skipped lines whenever I read. I would start by trying to follow the printed words in a book. Then, after a few seconds, the space between the lines turned into a flowing, white river. I'd try to come back to the letters, but the current of the white space was too strong.

I tried to explain this to Zahra, who sat next to me in class.

"Do you see the white river?" I asked her. She didn't. I looked back down and saw that the river had dried up and the space had become the dusty roads that lead from Ramsar to Tehran. I was fascinated by my discovery.

A year later, my stepfather was still without a job and we were still stranded in Ramsar. That meant seeing Mrs. Rushanas again each day. There wasn't a class that went by in which someone didn't get hit. Each time the blow seemed fiercer than the last one. Usually, the first five people she brought to the front of the class got it the worst: she had more energy earlier in the day. One morning, a classmate rushed into class, shaking, before Mrs. Rushanas arrived. The student could hardly put her words together.

"I saw her!" the girl yelled, out of breath. "She cut a branch from a tree."

We all sat down in our seats as fast as we could and tried not to move. The class was so quiet that I could hear the different rhythms of each person's heartbeat; together they sounded like a band starting up a song. Then I heard Mrs. Rushanas's steps coming toward the room—heavy, rhythmic—like a bass drum sounding beneath the high rattle of our little hearts.

The beat is infectious. Listen. All the kids are out of their seats, dancing on their desks. Mrs. Rushanas has taken off her headscarf and tied it around her hips, like a belly dancer. See how she shimmies and shakes! She's actually beautiful: her soft hair matches her hazel eyes. And she has a great smile. This morning, for the first time, you can see it.

"Stop looking at me like that. Open your hands," Mrs. Rushanas said to me.

I was confused to find myself standing in front of her desk. Her scarf was pulled firmly over her head and around her jaw. There was no smile on her face. No one was dancing. Eight students were standing behind me in line, each one waiting her turn. Mrs. Rushanas held a long, thin switch in her hand.

"I didn't do anything wrong," I said.

"You're illiterate," she said. "Now give me your hands."

I did. She hit them with what seemed all her might. I started to cry.

"One," she said.

I tucked my hands into my armpits for relief. She looked impatiently at me and made a hurried gesture for me to put my hands out again. I did. Whack!

"Two. Three. Four . . . Ten." I turned away and sat down at my desk, sobbing.

Batool was next. She got hit longer and harder. But she didn't cry. Instead, she extended her palms out further toward Mrs. Rushanas, as if to say that her teacher's beatings weren't working. In response, Mrs. Rushanas said, "I will tame you like a horse."

Unlike other times that I'd been hit, I didn't disappear. My hands were bleeding and the pain wouldn't go away. But I couldn't seem to leave my body either.

You have to follow the pain. To see where it leads. Like a river. If you fight the current, it pulls you under. Just go with it.

At dinner my mother asked why I was holding the spoon with my fist. I showed her my hands, which still bore the marks of Mrs. Rushanas's switch.

"Who did that to you?" my mother asked, wild-eyed.

"My teacher."

"Well, what did you do?" she demanded.

"I don't know," I said. It was the truth. I couldn't remember what had led to the beating.

That night my brother told stories about his teacher, Mr. Mosharafi, who had apparently been hitting him in class as well. His stories seemed even more traumatic and awful than mine, and he looked forlorn as he told them. His voice was starting to change too, and he made little squeaks that added an additional sorrowful effect.

A lot has been written about the politics of Iran after the revolution, but as far as I know, no one has really written about the cruelty to children that occurred at that time. People were so destabilized, and many kids got the brunt of the insanity that was in the air, everywhere. People were angry, pent up, and above all, not free to express their sexuality. And yet, no one talks about how that translated into the mistreatment of children.

My mother listened to us calmly for a while, but then gradually began to talk to herself. This always meant something bad was about to happen. After dinner, she got up to wash the dishes, which was usually my responsibility, but this time she insisted. Clearly, my torn-up hands were worthless for that job. I saw her talking to the water.

"Those teachers are going to die," her lips said.

Sure enough, the next morning she showed up at my school. From my seat in class, I could hear her screaming at someone in the teacher's lounge down the hall. Then the shouting stopped. It sounded as though my mother hadn't found the right person to yell at. I heard the door of the lounge slam and my mother's footsteps walking down the hall. She started knocking on the door of every classroom calling, "Atash-joon! Atash-joon!" When she finally got to our class, I got up to let her know I was there. Mrs. Rushanas looked terrified. I was shaking too. Neither of us knew what my mother was about to do.

"Are you her teacher?" my mother asked Mrs. Rushanas, pointing vaguely in my direction. She was holding a big tree branch in her hand.

"Yes, I am," Mrs. Rushanas said. "Please calm down, ma'am. We are all here to help these children."

"If you touch my daughter again," my mother said. "I am going to kill you, cut you into tiny pieces, and feed them to stray dogs. Do you understand?" She shook her stick in Mrs. Rushanas's face some more. I sat still, waiting for something worse to happen. I closed my eyes, and when I opened them, I thought I saw my mother ripping Mrs. Rushanas's veil off her head and tearing out her hair. After a few minutes, Mrs. Rushanas was bald.

The Witch will tear herself apart with anger. Hide. It will soon be over.

"Open your eyes," my mother said. She took my hand and marched me out of the classroom. It was only as we were leaving that I turned back to look at Mrs. Rushanas. I was happy to see that her scarf was still on her head and that her hair was intact. *What is happening to my brain?* I thought. All the way home, I was haunted by my vision of a stripped, bald Mrs. Rushanas. This image would continue to come into my mind at various times over the next month. I didn't know what it meant, but I grew more anxious about it.

I'd been aware of my mother's rage since the day I was seven and she screamed at the judge in the courthouse, but I never saw her threaten anyone with a weapon. This was also the first time I'd seen her stick up for me without getting anything in return. I was confused, but I believed her completely when she said she was ready to kill. I think Mrs. Rushanas did too, because she never hit me again. In fact, she also stopped hitting my classmates. For months, when she got mad, she would hit her desk and make angry sounds. Sometimes she looked straight at me and ground her teeth. My classmates became very sweet to me. They shared their lunch with me and let me cheat off them during exams.

A few weeks later, my mother asked how things were at school. I told her there hadn't been any beatings, but I didn't tell her about the white roads and rivers in my books. I remembered my father's family expressing concern over my mother's "craziness" and how she might pass her insanity onto her children. The last person I wanted to talk about the white roads and dancing letters with was my mother.

"Good," my mother said. "Now I need you to do something for *me*." She gave me two huge trash bags filled with clothes and a sheet with prices written on it to bring to school.

"Take these to Mrs. Rushanas. She'll know what to do with them," my mother said.

I did as I was told. When I got to school, Mrs. Rushanas took the bags from me soberly. She asked me to go to class and make everyone be quiet. I followed her instructions, pleased that I had been chosen as the monitor.

I later found out the significance of those clothing bags. Apparently, my mother had continued bullying Mrs. Rushanas and had coerced her into selling the clothes from my stepfather's final shipment to the other teachers and staff at my school. At the end of the day, Mrs. Rushanas handed me a large stack of cash and told me to say hello to my mother for her. I transported the clothes and money, back and forth between home and school, for several weeks. We bought groceries, and finally had many new, delicious meals.

My mother's "friendship" with my teacher didn't change my fears at school, however. Reading was becoming more and more scary. Now, whenever I opened a book, the letters would explode like confetti in the air and I had to slam the cover shut to keep from getting covered in ink. The words were like characters in a cartoon too: some would hiss at me or yell; others would giggle. I remember how the letter *n*, which in Persian is written with a half circle, would become a full circle and grow a stick underneath it, like a ping-pong paddle. The paddle would then start swatting at me and try to smack the center of my forehead. I'd shut my book with a bang, and everyone in class would stare at me—especially Mrs. Rushanas, whose piercing eyes told me she was waiting for her moment of revenge.

When I think back to my struggles with learning, I'm struck by how often teachers called me *khar*—"donkey." I was afraid of that word, which also meant shame in having to carry someone else's burden of judgment like a pack animal. I was amazed when I came to America and found there were words for what I was experiencing that didn't feel so violent: "processing disorder" or, more accurately, "dyslexia." What's more, some children who were like me in America even got a second teacher!

I've spent so much of my life trying to hide my dyslexia. As a writer, I live with the constant fear that someone will find my journals and discover how many spelling mistakes my unedited thoughts contain. And though I love books, I also go through periods when it's very hard for me to stare at words on a page. In grad school, I solved this problem by inviting my classmates over for dinner whenever we had a test and asking them to summarize chapters of the textbook while I cooked us delicious Persian food. They always thanked me, and I never had to face that river of words alone.

One day in sixth grade, I came late to class and I found several students lined up in front of the room, just like in the old days.

"Have a seat, Miss Atash," Mrs. Rushanas said nastily. "I might not be able to hit you, but I can hit them."

She hit every single person in class that day except me. I was crying the whole way through the ordeal. I kept asking her to stop, but she wouldn't.

"They are getting *your* share," she said.

Needless to say, from that day on, almost every student hated me once again. I kept a low profile and spent time with only my two other outcast friends, Zahra the little person and Batool the rich girl.

A few weeks later, it was time for spring cleaning, or *khooneh takooni* (shaking the house). In Iran, just before the first day of spring, people of all ages take time to go to parks, streets, and other outdoor spaces to pick up litter, plant flowers and trees, and collectively make their environment more beautiful in time for the vernal equinox, which is also the Persian New Year.

Mrs. Rushanas and the other teachers took us out into the schoolyard and instructed us to gather rocks and move them into the corners of the yard. It was strenuous work, but I was delighted not to have to do any reading that day. Zahra had a doctor's note that exempted her from lifting; she sat in the corner and watched the other girls. Batool and I worked together carrying the bigger rocks. It was a beautiful day and everyone was happy to be outside. Then I felt a painful sensation in my back. I turned around and saw a few girls holding rocks as big as grapefruits. They were throwing them at me. One hit my chest and another my head.

"Ugly Tehrani," they said. "We hate you. You have to leave our school and our lives."

More rocks hit me. I felt a dizzying sensation in my temples and the warmth of blood streaming down my face. Then everything went black.

You became a river. You tried to run away, but that just led you closer to the Witch. We found you, diverted your course, and gathered you here. Now you are a hidden pool. You feel calm because no one can trouble you.

When I woke up in the hospital, my head was shaved, and a bandage covered twenty stitches. I didn't remember the procedure. The doctors and nurses said I had been unconscious for most of the day. Then I heard my mother crying in the hallway.

"Her brain is already damaged," I heard her say. "How much worse will she get?"

I didn't feel that bad, honestly, though my head hurt a lot. I could see that all my friends from the House of Stone had come to the hospital with flowers and sweets and were sitting in a ring around me. It was nice to have them there.

My mother came back into the room.

"Atash, who are you talking to?"

"Nobody, Mommy," I lied. "Why?"

"This happened to you because of your name, Atash," she said. "I always knew that your name would bring us nothing but bad luck."

I looked at her. *Maybe she's right*, I thought. I could use a new name. A fresh start.

"I want to change your name to Aram," she said. *Aram* means "calm" in Persian.

This wasn't the first time my mother had brought up "Aram" as a new name for me, but I had always ignored her before. Now, there was a part of me that liked the idea of being someone else. She reminded me of how she changed her name when she married my stepfather and insisted that everyone call her "Soraya," instead of her real name.

"My old name belongs to your father," she'd said. "It's Soraya who will make her new husband happy." *Maybe it's better to have different names to go with different parts of life*, I thought.

My mother took me to City Hall to have my name changed several times, but something always went wrong. Once, the line was too long. Another time, the clerk never came back from lunch. After a while, my mother stopped talking about "Aram." But I remembered her. She's one of my parts, and I will carry her inside me forever.

When I was finally healed enough to go back to school, it was time to start junior high, in the new building directly adjacent to my old elementary school. The two schools shared a wall, and sometimes I could still hear Mrs. Rushanas beating the fifth graders next door. I looked for Batool and Zahra, but they were gone. I found out that Batool had moved away and that Zahra had died in her sleep that summer. I know that her medical condition was the reason for her death, but I still felt as though she partly died of shame from having to sit in Mrs. Rushanas's trash can. I wished so badly that I'd been brave enough to pull her out of the trash can in front of the teacher. I fantasized that, by standing up for her, I could have helped her live longer.

When I was a school social worker, I dealt with bullying among students a lot. To be honest, it was always easy for me to see both sides. Once, I confronted a tall girl who kept blocking a short girl from passing her in the hall. In just a few minutes of talking to the tall girl, I learned that she had been bullied in the same way too. It's not hard for me to see how these cycles get perpetuated, and I can have compassion for every child involved. But to this day, if I see an adult bullying a child, my compassion goes out the window and I feel an old rage well up inside me.

Surprisingly enough, my reading problems lessened when I was in sixth grade, though I was always still afraid that the letters would begin dancing again. Something new happened, though, that was even scarier. Now, whenever I read, there was a part of me that was calm, detached, and unafraid of getting into trouble or making mistakes: this part of me was Aram. But at other times, whole schooldays would go by, and when the last bell had rung, I realized I couldn't remember anything that had happened that day. I also noticed that sometimes, when I looked at my classmates' faces, they seemed like total strangers. Some of the girls who had put me in the hospital smiled at me as though we were best friends. I didn't really even remember being at the hospital at that point, to be honest.

I started keeping notes on all my classmates, complete with diagrams of where they sat, what they looked like, and even what their names were. I started keeping lists and crib sheets for everything in my life: the people I met, where I hid my allowance, what clothes I owned. Some days, when I got dressed, I put on clothes that weren't mine. I was afraid that I'd been stealing clothes without even knowing it. One time, when we were getting dressed up for a holiday, my mother found her blouse in my closet.

"Just ask me before you take it next time, okay, Atash?"

I had no memory of taking it.

Another time, I found myself in a math competition. I didn't think I could do math to save my life, but apparently I'd been accepted to compete. I looked around and saw six girls in front of me, separated at a distance from each other. I studied the booklet in front of me and couldn't make sense of any of it. So I got up slowly, walked to the front of the class, and handed the booklet to the woman by the door.

"Are you finished?" she asked.

"Yes," I said.

"But you didn't finish the last page. You have to answer all the questions in order to win."

"I'm finished," I said and ran out.

Nowadays, when I find myself in an unfamiliar place, I don't run. I know I'm in that place probably because a part of me signed up for something it really wanted to do. So I stay, try not to panic, and wait for that part to come back and take over.

There were so many days that I came home with new pens, notebooks, lipsticks, and other things that didn't belong to me. Or did they? All I knew was that time kept slipping from my grasp and that, if I was going to live a normal life, I was going to have to hide my forgetting from the world.

That was the hardest year of my childhood, because, for the first time, I became aware that I was hardly ever aware.

A month after the math competition, my mother asked if I would like a party for my thirteenth birthday. I didn't have any friends, and people at school didn't like me, but my mother said, "Throwing a party is *how* you make friends. You feed them and show them a good time, and then they like you." I couldn't remember the last time I'd had a birthday party—certainly before the revolution—so I said yes enthusiastically. The next day, when I went to school, I invited forty of my classmates, hoping I'd get ten to come. To my surprise, everyone said yes. I felt amazing. I was that girl who sat in the back of the room, cried to herself, and stared at walls. But now, I would be accepted.

My birthday arrived, and the tables in my house were set. My mother made three different dishes: eggplant with lamb, Persian herb stew, and saffron barberry rice. Between the red of the berries, the green of the herbs, and the yellow of the flowers, there was an explosion of color in our usually drab home. I wore a white dress with red flowers embroidered on it. It was a little big for me, but I thought it made me look pretty.

"You can't say you're not special now," my brother remarked.

At four o'clock, I stood by the door, waiting for the guests to arrive. Everything was very still.

The clock changed to 4:30. Then to 5:00, 6:00, 6:30, 7:00.

I knew something was wrong, but I couldn't move from the doorway. My legs seemed stuck to the ground. Then I heard my mom's nervous laugh, a sign that things were very bad.

"Atash-joon," she said. "The party is beginning. Please sit down and eat."

As I sat next to her and looked down at the long row of empty chairs, I felt warm tears fall down my face. My mother turned to me and glared.

"This is the party *I* made for you," she said. "You will not ruin it with your crying."

Just then, Maman Bozorg, who was visiting from Tehran, came in and sat down across from me.

"On your birthday," she said, "you have special wishing powers. It doesn't matter that no one came today. Don't let go of your wishing powers. Use them wisely and pray for good things for you and everyone you know."

I closed my eyes and thought: *What is it that I want more than anything?*

To get as far away from here as possible.

10

WHITE

I'm White. The other girls had to translate the words you are reading right now into English because I'm not good with language like they are. Inside the House of Stone, I know every tongue and can read a book like anyone else, but outside, words turn into rivers that carry me downstream to the Witch and her volcano.

I used to wander freely in the forest. One of my favorite things to do was watch the squirrels store nuts and try to memorize how many were hidden in different holes. I'm good with numbers and have an excellent memory.

One day, though, I became aware that someone was watching me. He was a short man who wore a black hood and carried a long knife. At first, I thought he was hunting for food in the forest, but he never came closer or moved farther away than a hundred yards from me. He just followed me around, watching. Gradually, my games with the squirrels turned into figuring out the best places to hide from him.

But he always found me and continued to stare.

One time, I saw him across a small ravine and decided to speak to him.

"Who are you? Why do you keep looking at me?"

He seemed startled by my voice. He stepped back from me and sat on some nearby tree roots. Then he started to cry, softly.

"Why are you crying?" I called out to him. "How do you keep finding me? Did the Witch send you?"

"Yes," he said through tears. "But I don't love her. It's you I love."

"You don't know me," I said. "Also, you're very old."

His wrinkled face twisted into a scowl.

"Love doesn't understand age," he said.

It suddenly occurred to me that I had no reason to stay. "I have to get going," I said to the hunter. "Please don't find me anymore."

"I will always find you," he said. "I can smell you from across the forest."

I got up to leave, but somehow he appeared behind me, as though his body had teleported across the ravine. He was holding me in his arms. I started to scream.

"Please don't struggle," he said. "You'll only make it worse."

And that's when it happened. I was thinking of all the words I wanted to say to him, all the words that wouldn't come out of my mouth, and all of a sudden the words started to flow like a river. I looked down at my body and saw it had turned clear as water. I looked at my arms and legs and torso and saw that their shape had started to run. I felt my body pour into the ground. I heard sounds echoing through the forest, but I was nowhere, spread out in a puddle across the earth.

Gradually, I became aware of two women talking above me. "How do you feel?" one of them said to me.

"Calm," I said. "But I don't know where or what I am. I can't feel my body."

"You became a river," one said. "You tried to run away, but that only led you closer to the Witch. We found you and diverted your course and gathered you here. Now you're a hidden pool. You feel calm because no one can trouble you."

I didn't understand. "But when will I get my old body back?" I asked.

"In this world, you can't," the other woman said. "Or at least, we don't know how yet. But you're safe, and we are with you."

Minutes became hours, hours melted into days, then days became weeks. I stopped counting. Gradually, I settled into the deepest calm I'd ever known. Sometimes I heard the voices of children playing around me. Sometimes I heard the sounds of women sobbing. I received them all as my sisters and shared my peace with them.

I know there's more to my story, but I don't know the rest yet. Maybe you, who are better with words than I am, can figure out where this stream is carrying me.

11

ALL ABOUT MY SUITORS

My mother assigned house chores to everyone according to age. She was always in charge of cooking, while my sister, Ava, who was about five at this time, set the table. I was now in charge of making salad and washing the dishes. My brother had to take out the trash. My stepfather cleared the dishes when we'd finished eating and prepared the after-dinner tea. Everyone seemed happy about the responsibilities meted out by my mother, except me, who never liked washing dishes. I still don't, though I've noticed in recent years that I love delegating tasks and making sure that teams of people work together smoothly. Some people might think I'm bossy, but it's a practical issue for me: I never know when I'll lose track of time, so I want to get systems in place and gears turning before the plan changes.

We always had a guest or two for dinner, usually someone who was of potential financial help to the family. My mother insisted we make our guest feel special by serving him food and tea and not letting him help with the cleanup.

"*Na zaar bi-siyah o sefid dast bi-zanand*," she'd insist, which means, "Don't let the guest touch anything between black and white." In other words: make sure he stays seated like a fat king at the table.

After dinner one night, when everyone had thanked my mother for her delicious meal, one of the guests kept complimenting my mother to the point of exhaustion. He went on and on, saying that her cooking skills were not of this world.

"I envy you," he told my stepfather. "You get to eat like this every day."

The hostility behind my stepfather's smile was unbearable. I got up to go to the kitchen and start washing dishes. When we had guests, my mother used fancy china, which meant more time for me at the kitchen sink. It took almost an hour to finish, so I tried to make the best of that time by singing some songs by Googoosh, my favorite singer. I loved a particular song of hers called "Tu-yi yek divareh-sangi" (In a Stone Wall). That night I sang it over and over again as I washed. It was about two windows trapped in a stone wall who cannot touch each other. Love is like that, Googoosh seemed to be saying. "Only in death is there true freedom," she softly sang.

Just then, I felt warm hands pressing on my neck, then on my shoulders, bringing a familiar nausea back to my stomach.

"I like it when you put your hair up like that. It makes your neck look nice," my stepfather said.

"Thank you," I said and deepened my focus on the dishes.

"You are becoming a truly beautiful woman," he told me.

Then we heard my mother yell from the living room, "Is the tea ready?"

"Just a second!" he yelled back. I felt his breath still on my neck.

"You smell good too," he said. He was sniffing like a dog.

My mother yelled again, and my stepfather stepped back. He picked up the tray of tea and turned for the living room.

I went on washing in silence, listening to my own heartbeat. I became aware of my own forgetting. *He does this a lot,* I realized. *Why do bad things keep slipping out of my mind? Then, when they happen again, I know they've happened many times before. And then they're gone again.*

He's not a problem. He's too pathetic to hurt you.

I thought of an image of being six years old and sitting in my stepfather's lap. My mother used to say, "I married him because I saw you liked him, Atash. Whenever he'd come over you'd run over and climb into his arms."

But now I remembered something else: the hardness I felt under me as I sat in his lap. It seemed connected to a lot of other hard, painful things. Lately, my brother had been punching me in the chest, which hurt more than usual. I remembered other flashes of men's hard parts. The idea of becoming a woman felt dangerous, like getting hit with rock.

Suddenly I saw red liquid in the water in front of me. I'd cut my hand.

"Ooooow!" I screamed, though I couldn't actually feel the pain. Saying it just felt like what I was supposed to do.

My mother ran into the kitchen. "What's going on here?" she yelled.

"She cut herself again," my stepfather told her, arriving just behind her.

My mother shook her head. "When are you going to grow up?" she asked. "You can't even wash dishes right. Leave it. I'll do them myself." Then she looked at my cut. "It doesn't look too bad," she said in a softer tone. "Better than the other times." She found a Band-Aid and pressed it to my finger.

At that moment, I realized Ava had been standing in the doorway of the kitchen for some time. She was staring at her father with a puzzled expression, as though she were trying to figure something out. My stepfather noticed her too and looked alarmed. "*Shab bikhayr*, Baba," she said to him. "Good night, Daddy."

"Why are you still up?" he asked her.

"I want to go up with Atash."

I took her little hand and led her upstairs to the bedroom we shared. Ava was clinging tightly to me as we walked together. She was terrified of the dark and used to be able to fall asleep only with the light on. She suffered from night terrors that year, so she rarely slept in her own bed, preferring to share mine with me, which was bigger, anyway. I often lay next to her and told her stories. Her big eyes would beam, and she looked really cute in the old T-shirt of mine she wore as a nightgown. I'd scold her that it was time to go to sleep, and she'd close her eyes, but a few moments later a little flutter of her lids told me she was just pretending. Sometimes I fell asleep in the middle of my own story and woke beside her at dawn.

Ava and I got closer that year. I don't know how much she— or I, for that matter—understood about the changes that were happening to me, but I thought of her as my little guardian angel. I protected her from the teasing of older kids, and she, in turn, seemed to keep me safe just by being there. In her company, bad things just didn't happen.

I was so speechless and timid in those days—nothing like how I am now: someone who actually looks forward to necessary confrontations. I remember noticing the change in me years later, in New York City, when I got on a subway car and noticed three women sitting together with that terrified look I knew so well. I sat down next to them, not knowing exactly what was happening but feeling their panic and freeze all the same.

After a minute, I noticed a tall man with sunglasses lean forward toward our group. He lifted his arm to grab the rail above, and as his hand went up, so did his T-shirt, revealing his penis hanging over the top of his belt, less than a foot from my face. The bodies of the women around me crumpled, but I knew exactly what he wanted: our fear. I felt rage rise, first in my feet, then in my throat, and I said loudly, in the best English I could muster, "FIX YOURSELF," and stomped on his feet with my boot, surprising even myself with the volume of my voice. The man didn't react, so I said it again, "FIX YOURSELF! FIX. YOUR. SELF!" His hand came down just as the subway doors opened, and he ran.

From that night when I cut myself at the sink, Ava insisted on staying up until I took her to bed. She even volunteered to help me dry dishes so we could finish sooner. Even though she was five then, she had a curious way of being with me that was almost maternal. I was grateful for her help and found her a chair so she could stand next to me by the sink. We used to laugh as we did the dishes, playing with the bubbles. My stepfather would come in and yell at her for getting her clothes wet, but we didn't care. We made faces at him when he wasn't looking and giggled together like kids of her age.

My mother never let on that she knew about my stepfather's behavior, but she must have seen how he changed with me. He used to stare at me throughout breakfast as he pretended to read the paper. He'd follow me as I got on the bus to school. I saw how he got into a cab and tailed the bus, how he would hide behind a tree when classes were done. Sometimes, I used to mess with him by getting off the bus a few stops early, running through a side alley, and getting on another bus. I'd still beat him home. He'd arrive out of breath and scream to my mother, "She's up to something! She has a boyfriend, I know!"

One night, while I was studying on the floor of my room, using my bed as a desk, he came in and sat down behind me on the floor. "I've been listening to your phone calls to that scrawny boy," he said.

His breath smelled like death. My fingers felt the sharp tip of the pen I was writing with.

Put it in his neck.

Then I felt him come closer. His whole body was now pressed to mine. I could feel his hard penis against my back.

"Don't think you're slick," he whispered. "I know everything you do with him. Do you think I raised you so that he could have you?"

I felt the pen in my hand again. I really wanted to use it, but a force outside of me kept me from turning around. I also noticed a presence from over to my left. I turned and saw my mother standing in the doorway. She didn't say anything. She just turned and walked away. Gradually, my stepfather got up and left too.

The next day she said at the breakfast table, "You're almost fourteen, Atash. It's time for you to think about marriage. I'm going to start asking around for eligible suitors."

That night in bed, I noticed how bad I smelled. It was after ten, but I really couldn't stand the odor of my own body. On my way to the shower, I heard my stepfather also complain to my mother about how filthy I'd become. That put a smile on my face. I turned around and went back to bed without washing.

Gradually, I stopped brushing my teeth as well. When my stepfather came near, it gave me great pleasure to think about how awful my mouth smelled. My mother noticed my deteriorating hygiene too.

"You're an embarrassment for our family!" she'd wail. "Who likes a filthy girl?"

And I'd giggle and reply, "No one, Mommy! No one!"

Once, she tricked me into going to a *hamaam*, one of those open public baths that exist throughout the Middle East. She had told me we were going shoe shopping but then insisted that first we had to stop at this gruesome spot in Katalom. We went into a miserable stone building whose hallway was dark and damp. Behind the desk, I saw three skinny old ladies. I had heard from other kids at school that these women were known for the aggressive way they scrubbed girls. My mother paid a few of these hags to clean me.

"Good luck," she told them, as she left me in their care.

"We'll make her shine like glass," one of them with missing teeth promised.

They took me into a steam room and asked me to take off my clothes and lie down on the slab to be washed and scrubbed.

"I'm not taking off a thing," I told them.

They surrounded me and began to strip me by force. I struggled, but eventually they won. As my clothes came off and the smell of my body filled the ancient stone room, they began to gag. But they didn't stop. One held me down while the other pushed shampoo into my thick hair. For a moment, the citrus smell made me remember something from a happy time, but I pushed the thought from my mind and kept fighting. They dodged my punches and went on, now conditioning and untangling my hair. I started to feel myself drifting, and my body relaxed.

When I came back into my body, I heard them talking about me as though I weren't in the room. I couldn't see them through the fog of the hamaam, but I heard their voices say:

"She's a beautiful girl."

"Yes, though it was hard to tell at first with all that dirt."

"What would make a young girl want to be so filthy?"

That got my attention. I'd never heard anyone ask *why* I did the things I did. Even now, sometimes, when I realize it's been days since I've thought about taking a shower, I have to stop and ask myself: "Why am I doing this? What am I trying to keep away?"

I began to cry. I cried and cried till I had no more water in my body and they'd finished. Then, one of the ladies took my chin, raised it, and said, "Don't be sad. You're young and have the rest of your life ahead of you. You never know what the future will bring."

This got the other ladies philosophizing. "If I were her age again," the lady with missing teeth said, "I'd go to college and become a doctor." The others laughed at this, and all three started to talk about their joys and regrets. They'd obviously forgotten about me. Pretty soon they were all laughing, and I was laughing along with them too.

My mother saw my lack of hygiene as the result of misdirected libido. She was convinced that if I started to think about marriage, and men, I would naturally take more interest in my own cleanliness. But I knew she just wanted me out of the house.

"Think about how happy you'll be in your fancy new home," she'd say, trying to get me to dream along with her about the man who'd sweep me off my feet.

She started to pack my schedule with *khastegari*—"meetings with suitors." At one point, she had me meet as many as three men a week. I discovered that I could usually get rid of these bidders by acting insane until they left. Sometimes, I'd blow huge bubbles with my gum in rapid succession, or burp loudly, or scratch myself all over as though I had fleas. This would enrage my mother, but there wasn't anything she could do when the suitor would get up and say, "It was truly a pleasure meeting your beautiful daughter, ma'am," and bolt for the door.

One particular day, my mother told me, "There's a man coming tomorrow." And then—as if to warn me that she had a plan—she said, "It will be different this time." The following day, she got up early and cleaned the whole house. She washed clothes, dusted furniture, watered the plants, and vacuumed the Shirazi carpets. She danced around the house, singing songs she invented: "My daughter's gone. She's gone to a riiiich man's house."

"I'm still a kid," I told her. "What's the rush?"

"You're a woman now," she said. "Please note that our schedule for today has two suitors on it."

Suitor #1 looked older than my father. When I saw how decrepit he was, I immediately stormed into the kitchen on the pretense of making him and his buttoned-up, long-sleeved, headscarf-wearing family some tea. Alone in the kitchen, I found one of my mother's cigarettes and began to smoke it. It was disgusting, and I started to cough violently. The suitor's sister heard the sound and came in. She was wearing all black and showed absolutely no hair under her chador.

"Oh," she asked innocently when she saw me standing there. "You smoke?"

"No, not really," I said, but then I thought about her ancient brother waiting for me in the other room.

"Actually, I do smoke," I said. "Lots and lots of cigarettes. Every day."

I watched her go back into the living room. I counted to thirty, in which time, I figured, she'd have notified her brother to leave. They did, with my distraught mother trailing behind them all the way to their Mercedes, begging them to say what had gone wrong.

A few hours later, our house bell rang. Suitor #2. My mother had asked me to fry some potatoes and act as though I was the one preparing lunch, presumably so the man at the door could imagine a future in which he would be fed by me. I hadn't started frying them yet, though, so when I heard the bell, I ran to the kitchen to make up for lost time. If I must marry, I thought, at least let him be young, handsome, and fun. I begged God as I stared out the window trying to catch a glimpse of him, "Please let him not be fifty again."

There were about eight people in the courtyard down below, all of them older. I couldn't tell which one was the suitor. My mother crept into the kitchen and whispered in my ear, "They are here. They are rich," and walked out again. *How does she know if they have money or not?* I wondered. It sounded as though everyone outside was laughing. I could hear them talking, but I couldn't make out what they were saying. I noticed that I felt a deep sense of obligation to at least prepare tea for the guests. I wasn't sure how many glasses to prepare, but I guessed about ten. I felt sick to my stomach.

There's a part of me that wants to hide from people, but there's also a part that loves to perform. I think a lot of Iranian women have this split. For them, *khastegari* is a kind of performance in which they are given a chance to shine, but it also can be an unpleasant ritual of being under a microscope, as the suitor's family examines the girl's face, body, and manners.

I still see this split in myself. For example, I now love to host large dinner parties—but for years, I wouldn't let myself serve anyone, ever, even if they were friends. It probably took a decade of partners and friends cooking for me before I realized that I was actually jealous of their role and wanted to be the one cooking and serving again. *This split is about being able to choose, I realized.*

My mother realized I felt ill and assured me everything would be okay. She went to the cabinet and brought out a long silver tray and set tiny glasses on it. She placed the tray in my hands and said, "Breathe . . . and smile." Then she pushed me out into the living room. I walked, looking at my tray, counting my steps, hoping I wouldn't drop anything. The glasses were packed tightly together and rattled loudly as I marched forward. When I got to the couches, I felt relieved. I put the heavy tray on the table with downcast eyes.

"*Salaam*," I said, but I wasn't sure if the word actually came out. Without looking up, I counted ten sets of feet. I approached the first. "*Befarmayeed*," I said. "Please take one." I went around this way till I reached the pair of feet I knew belonged to the suitor. I knew this because, when I arrived, the room became absolutely still.

"*Salaam, Atash-khanom*," the owner of the feet said in a pleasant voice.

"*Salaam bar shoma*," I replied.

The kindness of his voice gave me the confidence to raise my eyes. He was wearing black pants and a white shirt. Definitely handsome. He looked to be in his late thirties, which felt way too old for me, but he was the best—and youngest—I had met so far. I wasn't sure what to do, but I knew everyone was looking at me. My mother began to "work it" from the other side of the room. "Such a handsome man! If I were young again, I would certainly say yes to you." Then she cackled to a silent room.

When the last glass had been offered, I got up to carry the tray back to the kitchen. I saw that one of the suitor's uncles was having difficulty returning his glass to the table, so I walked over to help him. As I did, I passed a large fan set up in the corner of the room. I reached for the old man's glass, and then it happened. Everyone in the room made a collective "Ugggh," and their faces contracted in an expression of disgust.

"Your skirt! Your skirt flew up!" my stepfather hissed at me under his breath, and I knew I'd messed up big time.

Everything from then on went in slow motion. It felt like my feet were stuck in mud. When I finally got out of the room and into the kitchen, I realized I needed a bathroom, quickly. There was a burning sensation in my bladder. The bathroom, however, was on the other side of the house and could only be accessed through the living room. So I walked out and tried to say a quick, nonchalant hello to the guests as I passed. Their gazes hit me like a fist colliding with my bladder. I couldn't control the pressure, and there was nothing I could do to keep myself from peeing right there except to put my hand between my legs and walk like a crab across the room. If there had been any doubt up till that point, the sight of the suitor's potential bride holding her crotch as she sidled off officially broke the deal.

That wasn't smart. You have to use opportunities, not push them away. This is how we can cross the ocean and be safe. Don't make the same mistake next time.

12

GRAY

I'm Gray. In Persian, the word for "gray" is *khakestari*, which means literally "color of dirt," but I'll explain about that later. I don't sleep much, because of my night terrors, so my face has become gray too. I don't care. I'm glad I scare people. I'm ready to kill any motherfucker who tries to get inside these walls.

The other girls here are naive. They don't see that the Witch has been on to us for a long time. The hunter too. They only hear what they want to hear. If they took time, as I have, to sit by the White Pool and listen to what she says, they'd know the hunter has been close for many weeks now. He finds us by smell. I don't know how, but we have some scent that draws him to us.

I was out with Green helping her gather herbs when I realized he was following us. I didn't tell Green, because she's too sweet to deal with someone like him, but I made sure we followed a fake path to put him off our trail. I told Green I wanted to see one of the caves where Blue plays sometimes. Then, when we were out of sight, hidden among the rocks, I told Green I'd forgotten something and had to turn back. My maneuver confused the hunter and also made sure he'd come to the caves again looking for me.

That night, I waited among the rocks for his return. In my hand, I held a knife I'd stolen from the kitchen. I charged at him before he could figure out what was happening and stabbed him in the heart. But when my blade pierced his chest, there was no heart or even blood beneath his skin, only empty space. I yanked the knife out in horror and ran off.

I had to get rid of our scent. There was no other method of keeping the hunter away. It was hot in those days—summer— and I convinced the other girls that the best way to keep cool was to cover their skin with mud. "Like elephants," I said, and the little ones liked that idea. I gathered ashes from the fireplace, mixed them with dirt and water, and we smeared ourselves, like women in mourning.

But it was no use. The summer heat had reached a breaking point, and storms were gathering. Within a few hours, our mountain was drenched in rain, which beat its way through the windows and doors. Water came up through the sink drains, and all the ashes were washed away. In the morning, when we woke to find Burgundy putting our broken furniture back together and bailing water from the bedrooms, we all smelled like sunshine and pine trees. I knew we had to flee and take our House with us, but I had no idea where to go.

Hopeless, I sat by the White Pool and cried and cried. At some point, I heard Green nearby, talking to her plants. They were telling her about life on something called the Far Island. I asked Green about this island, and she told me it's where the seabirds lay their eggs and that I should talk to them if I want to learn more. So I went down to the shore with pistachios and walnuts to offer the birds in exchange for information. From their stories, I pieced together a few different possible maps of the Far Island and its distance from our House. I didn't want to tell the others what I was doing, so I hid the maps in folders with the names of famous film stars on them: Clark Gable, James Dean, Amitabh Bachchan, and so on. Whenever one of the girls asked me about the folders, I said, "Those are files I keep on the men I'm going to marry one day." They thought I was ridiculous and didn't pry any further.

13

HER & HIM

The "scrawny boy" my stepfather accused me of seeing secretly was Reza. He wasn't actually my boyfriend, but we did have an important connection. For the first year, we just stared at each other from afar without talking. I first noticed him at the sprawling beach near my school, where I went during recess or in the late afternoons to be alone and smoke a few loose cigarettes, which I stole from either my mother or brother, who had also started smoking.

Reza sometimes sat on the sand and smoked too; other times, he'd skip large rocks across the waves. I pretended not to know he was there, but I saw how patient he was, taking his time to find the best rocks to skip. He got so good that sometimes his rocks would jump ten times before they sank. The first time that happened, I felt inexplicably happy, so I jumped up and cheered. He noticed me cheering, and I remembered we were still strangers, so I sat back down on the sand and pretended nothing had happened. But Reza wasn't put off. He waved at me and I waved back, sheepishly, happy to be busted.

Our waving game went on this way for months, but any time Reza actually tried to walk toward me, I'd get up and run. The truth is, I didn't know what I'd say to him if we were to meet. I loved our love games from a distance. All I needed to know was that he noticed me, and I liked being a mystery, rather than a reality, to him. *I'm a sad girl*, I thought. Better he doesn't know.

One time I went to the beach and didn't find him. I came back the next day, and the next, and the next, hoping he'd return. I tried to learn to skip rocks the way he did, but it didn't come easily. Sometimes I saw other men there, but they were different from Reza: they'd come to the beach to smoke hashish and whistle at girls like me. "Hey sister, you want to smoke?" they'd yell, and when I declined, they'd change to a self-righteous tone: "What do you think you're doing here? This is not a place for nice girls."

I'd walk past them and act as though I were deaf. *The beach belongs to everyone*, I told myself, including girls, but I never saw other girls alone at the beach.

I always made sure to get home before sunset. My stepfather would be waiting, marching up and down in front of the house.

"Where have you been? Your mother and I were worried."

"I studied late in the school library with a friend," I'd lie. I don't think our school actually had a library.

"We know you're up to no good. You'll bring shame on our family one day."

He had no idea about my romantic life, of course. He assumed that if I came home fifteen minutes late, I'd been sleeping with thousands of men in that time. Or maybe he just liked to think those thoughts.

One day he informed me that he would be picking me up from school himself at exactly three o'clock.

"Are you going to watch me and my friends study too?" I baited him.

"*Zaboonet nish daareh*," he said, which means "Your tongue has a stinger," or, "Watch your mouth."

"Your friends can come here and study," my mother interjected.

"They won't," I said, and went up to my room.

As I went upstairs, I heard my mother say to my stepfather, "This is why we have to get her married quickly. She's out of control."

The next day I skipped my later classes and went to the beach around noon. I walked miles, sang Googoosh songs, and thought about Reza. I knew my stepfather would be waiting for me at three, but I wanted to mess with his head. So I took the bus home and arrived at six.

Both my mother and stepfather were at the front door waiting for me. He shoved me into the backseat of a cab, next to my mother, and climbed into the front seat. I heard him tell the driver to take us to an address in Shahsavar, the next town north of Ramsar.

"I can't make him stop his craziness," my mother whispered to me. "We're going to see a doctor and get a medical note confirming you are a virgin. We'll give it to your new suitors."

Panic set in. I remember all the blood from the man in Qom and the kid next door. *The doctor will know*, I thought. I remembered stories from religion class about girls who were stoned to death for having broken hymens. Who could I explain my situation to? Even if someone believed my stories, they'd think it was my fault anyway.

I stared out the window. I noticed that the trees were waving their branches. They looked like people in a theater clapping, and the sound of the wind rustling through them was like applause.

You're an actress. A wonderful actress. Your performance makes everyone happy. Sink into the role. Feel the applause.

My stepfather opened the back door of the taxi. I was shaking. Even the taxi driver nodded at me as though he knew what was about to happen. He looked at me with pity as he rolled his little window up and drove off.

The clinic was a run-down white building with lots of cars and ambulances parked out front. Inside, the space was very clean and nearly empty. I saw a sign that read "Detox Patients Here" and saw lots of young men, withdrawing from heroin, loitering around the main hall, smoking cigarettes. I thought about my uncle Hossain. No one seemed to know where he was in those days.

My mother approached the head nurse behind the counter. "Are you Ms. Mohamadian?" she asked. A young woman with a sweet smile said yes. Apparently the two had already had a long conversation.

Ms. Mohamadian came closer and introduced herself. "I am glad to meet you, Atash," she said. "That's your name, right? I'm the nurse here. The doctor is with a patient, but come with me into the back and we'll try to get you out of here as soon as possible." I was surprised how nicely she spoke to me. I half expected a witch to pick me up, throw me around, and tear off my clothes, like the old ladies at the public baths.

Twenty minutes later, I was sitting in an examination room facing the doctor. He was a large, hairy man with glasses, but he had a kind smile. As soon as he said hello, I started to sob.

"Please let me go," I cried. "I was hurt when I was a little girl by a man . . . I was hurt and my parents . . . "

"It's okay, dear," he interrupted me gently. "Here, have some orange juice."

I took the orange juice but didn't drink it. "I was hurt when I was a kid," I continued. "There was a lot of blood."

"I am sorry to hear that," he said. "How old were you?"

"Young. Please, I don't want to take off my clothes," I said and began to cry louder.

"You don't have to take off any clothes," he said, "But you need to keep a secret. I became a doctor to help people, not hurt them. Do you understand what I'm saying?"

I didn't, at least not completely.

"But my mother wants a note," I said.

"She will get her note," he said. "But I want you to understand that what was done to you was not okay."

I was getting frustrated. "I'm not a virgin!" I said at last.

"Atash," he said. "What happened to you has nothing to do with virginity. Losing your virginity is a choice you make when you're ready, not when you're a child."

He began to give me a long speech about *rezayat* (consent), speaking in a low voice so people outside couldn't hear. I'd never heard any adult in Iran talk like this before. I don't even remember most of what he said, because I was so overjoyed about the note he promised to give me. To be honest, I wasn't planning on ever having sex anyway—at least, not with boys—so his speech didn't concern me. I was aware of feeling excited when I looked at other girls in class and lingered on their skin and breasts, and the sound of their voice, but I had no idea what to do with that feeling. And yet, for some reason, I also still wanted to get closer to Reza.

"Finally," the doctor said, finishing his sermon, "I want you to keep this number on you at all times. For emergencies." He wrote a woman's name and telephone number on a piece of paper. "She's a surgeon," he said. "She helps girls like you. If they need to be sewn up again." I couldn't believe he was talking so openly.

Then he asked me, "Do you know how to act, Atash? Like in the movies?"

See? An actress, like in the movies.

"I don't know," I replied.

"Well, here's your chance," he said. "You just got an examination on this table, right? You didn't like it. No one does." He paused till I nodded my head.

"Hopefully next time they'll bring you here and not to another clinic," he said. "But you must make them think this was a horrible experience."

We walked out together and I put on the unhappiest face I could. The doctor asked me to sit in the waiting room while he talked to my parents in a separate room.

"I'm very sorry, Doctor," I heard my mother say, "but I think you've made a mistake. We're certain she's been with boys. Maybe when she was younger."

I started to tremble. So she knows?

"Can you examine her again?" my mother went on. "I'd be happy to accompany you."

"Are you questioning my credentials?" the doctor countered.

"Come on," I could hear my stepfather grumble. "We got the note."

"She can't be a virgin," my mother kept saying. "She can't."

"Ma'am," the doctor said, his voice rising, "you are playing a very dangerous game right now. And frankly, I'm beginning to believe it's you who needs a doctor."

"Come on!" my stepfather said again. Through the wall, I could hear the fear in his voice.

We were all silent on the way home. My stepfather looked straight ahead, but my mother kept smiling at me, as though I'd just won an award. I was so confused. A moment ago, she wanted to throw me to the wolves. Now, armed with a doctor's note, she was using it to stand up to my stepfather.

"I always said she was a good girl," my mother beamed from the backseat.

My stepfather said nothing, and neither did I.

Today, when a female student of mine tells me she doesn't want to "lose" her virginity, I can't help but ask, "Why do you think having sex is losing something?" It amazes me that, even in twenty-first-century America, young girls feel such a sense of struggle, and even sometimes failure, around deciding to have sex for the first time. It doesn't seem to matter what their ethnic or religious background is: the feeling is always the same sense of having fallen from grace. Even when I hear two girls calling each other "slut" in the hallways of my Manhattan school, my mind still travels back to that clinic in Shahsavar.

My stepfather stopped picking me up from school for a while after that doctor's visit, so I had a chance to visit the beach every day again, but I only stayed a short while now, since I didn't want to lose my privileges. I kept wondering if I'd ever get to see Reza again.

Finally, after six months of waiting, I literally ran into him in an alley that led down to the beach. I recognized him right away, though his hair had been shaved. This was the closest I'd been to him physically, and it made me happy to see that he was handsome after all. He had a round face with big brown eyes and long eyelashes. I've never met anyone with bigger eyes than me, but his were enormous. He looked at me with them, intensely and kindly. I looked at him too. He was wearing a military uniform, though I couldn't figure out whether it belonged to the army or one of the corrupt militias that were everywhere in those days. I slipped past him, trying not to be immodest, but as I passed, I turned to stare at him again.

"Wait," he said. "Don't you remember me?"

I decided to go for it. I motioned to him to follow me down to the beach. There, I picked up six smooth, flat rocks and gave him three. I skipped my first rock across the water: it made two jumps. I looked at him, smiled, and waited for him to follow my lead, but he just dropped his rocks onto the sand. He looked very serious.

"I knew you noticed me," he said. "I've thought about you so much. The morals police arrested me six months ago for nothing. And because I wasn't in college, they made me do military service. I didn't even get to say goodbye to my family. They took me straight to the Iraqi border."

He was talking rapidly now. His training had been intensive: before he knew it, he was on the front lines shooting a gun at Arabs. He'd seen dead people and all sorts of horrible things.

"I'm only home for three days," he said. "I have to go back to the front soon, but I'd like to write you letters. My name is Reza. Where do you live? What's your name?"

I didn't know which question to respond to first, so I said nothing. Then, finally, I said, "I have to go home. If I don't go home now, I'll never be able to see you again." I told him about my mother and stepfather, and how I never felt safe with them. He was the first person I ever spoke to about my situation. I trusted him, maybe because I knew he was going away.

He looked concerned but didn't seem to judge me. He held my hands with tears in his eyes. I took his address and gave him my phone number.

"Don't write to me at home," I said. "I'll write to you and tell you where to send the letters."

I didn't see him again for five months.

I've always secretly liked long-distance relationships. There's something about not having to be with people that allows me to think of them, miss them, and reassure myself that everything is okay. Even now, I leave my partners a lot to travel, and

I find that I actually enjoy missing them. That's how I know that what I have is precious. But if I'm honest, I think I also like the fact that long-distance relationships make me feel normal. When people I love are far away, they don't see me staring off into space for long periods of time, or misplacing important objects, or not remembering key facts about our relationship. I get to be free from all the reminders of what I don't understand about my own life.

A week later, my aunt, her husband, and her two college-aged sons came to stay with us for seven days. My aunt and mother, though sisters, weren't particularly close, but since Maman Bozorg had been getting older and frailer, we'd all started spending more time together by the sea.

My aunt brought me pretty pink boxes of gifts and called me her "beautiful bride," which was my first tip-off that she and my mother were plotting to marry me to her older son, my cousin Shahpour. I used to play with Shahpour when we were little, but I hadn't seen him since we moved to Ramsar. He was studying engineering at the University of Tehran, told really funny jokes, and knew how to breakdance to Michael Jackson's song "Thriller," which was playing on every boombox in Iran in those days. I liked hanging out with him. When I stood next to him, though, the thought of kissing him, let alone marrying him, seemed ridiculous. I wondered how he felt too. Maybe he felt grossed out by me too and was just playing along to please his mother.

Disgusted by their scheming, I left my gifts unopened in the living room. But eventually, my mother got curious about the boxes. She sat down with my aunt and opened each one herself, praising the jewelry, perfume, and makeup they contained.

"Atash isn't as rude as she seems," my mother said, knowing full well I could hear. "She's just a bit shy. Fifteen is a hard age. But once she's finished with high school, she'll make a wonderful bride."

That evening, some neighbor came by with flowers and congratulated my mother and aunt on the union they had arranged. *How many people know about this?* I wondered. The neighbor gave me a brief smile but didn't seem interested in me otherwise. I went to my room, but my stepfather kept coming in to check on me and ask how I was feeling. Since the episode with the doctor's note, he'd begun to act more paternal toward me. Having him in my room made me feel ill, however, so I went out onto the porch and spent the rest of the evening playing with my new black-and-white cat, Fandogh (Hazelnut). I talked to Fandogh about Turkey and Cyprus, the two countries that Iranians did not need a visa to visit. I told Fandogh, "Watch me, I'm going to leave this country after all. Maybe I'll take you too." Fandogh purred approvingly.

For the moment, though, I needed a conspirator to help me get Reza's letters. The trouble was I wasn't well liked, so my best bet seemed to be a classmate of mine named Shirin, whom everyone called "Hideous Girl." I didn't find Shirin ugly at all, but she was different. She dressed in boy's clothes, aside from her mandatory headscarf, and didn't take care of her hygiene very well. She had facial hair and smelled like I used to a few years before. This got me wondering whether we shared something in common. A few weeks after we met, I found out we did. I told her about my situation at home, and she told me that her uncle used to touch her. After that, we quickly became the best of friends.

One day during recess, I didn't go to the beach; instead, I sat in the schoolyard near the big tree that Shirin read under every day.

"What are you reading?" I asked.

"*Dorogh-e Bozorg*," she said, a title that translated to "The Big Lie." "It's a love story and it's banned."

"I only read books that are banned," I lied.

I offered her some of my lunch, and we ate together without talking. When the bell rang, we got up to go to class. In class, she asked me if I'd like to change my seat and sit next to her. I accepted and moved to the back, where she always sat to avoid the insults of other kids.

"I have a boyfriend," I told her. "He's a soldier. We don't talk or see each other much, but we like to skip rocks together."

She laughed. "How romantic," she said.

"Could you get his letters for me if he sends them to your place?"

She gave me a strange look, but she nodded.

Shirin and I hung out every day and even had sleepovers at my house. She warmed herself to my mother by giving her lots of compliments, washing our dishes, and helping with cooking and baking. I was happy to have a good friend and fewer responsibilities in the kitchen, but I was also a little jealous of my mother's attention to Shirin. My mother enlisted Shirin, as she did with everyone, to help convince me to marry Shahpour. She told Shirin that as an "adopted daughter," she had important responsibilities in this respect. Shirin also won over my sister Ava, who was now in grade school, by helping her with her school projects and reading her stories to help her fall asleep.

According to Shirin, her parents didn't mind that she stayed with us. She had seven or eight siblings, and I once heard my mother say, "They must be happy to feed one less person." At some point, Shirin was spending almost every night at our house and sleeping in my bed.

"I'm glad you found a family who loves you," I said to her one night. I think she understood the sarcasm in my voice.

"I don't care about their love, Atash," she said. "I want to be here with you. That's why I let them think I want to be their daughter too."

"My mother is using you against me and my wishes."

"Well, I'm not buying it," she said. "I know what she's doing and she knows that no one can make you say yes to getting married. They might force you into a wedding, but they know full well that when the imam comes, you can always tell him no and he'll be forced to stop the ceremony."

"I want out of this house," I said. "I can't get dressed up in white and go through all that just to say no. They'd kill me. I either have to get married or run away, and I can't marry my cousin, so I guess I have to run away."

"Maybe you could talk to your aunt and Shahpour individually and convince them that you're not the right bride."

"Don't you see, Shirin? There will just be another suitor, and another. I have to get out of this country. That's the only way. Besides, I'm failing all my classes too. There's no future for me here."

"That's crazy talk, Atash. Haven't you heard stories about what happens to runaway girls? You want the government to pick you up and marry you off to five rich mullahs a day?"

"What are you talking about, Shirin?"

"Don't you know about *sigheh*? They can force you to get 'married' for a few hours to each guy for money. Then where would you be? Once you belong to the government, no one can save you."

I'd never heard of this before. I was horrified, but I kept up my act. "No one is going to catch me," I said. "Will you help me find a way out?" But Shirin was tired of my scheming.

"Let's go to sleep, Atash. Come to bed."

We lay in bed together in silence. I felt a bit annoyed with Shirin for questioning my plan. I reached over to my bedside drawer, pulled out one of my mother's cigarettes I'd stolen from her earlier that day, and began to smoke. I fell asleep almost immediately after it was finished.

I woke up in the darkness of the night. I felt a soft touch on my inner thighs. Shirin was breathing heavily on my skin too. I didn't know what to do with what I was feeling, so I continued acting like I was asleep. I thought, *I'm not going to do anything. I'm going to see how far she takes this.* Shirin's hand began to move to the elastic of my underwear. Her fingers were sliding slowly across my belly and back down to my thighs again, like she was playing a soft song on a piano. It felt really good.

But then I imagined not being able to stop. I imagined Shirin covering my mouth and tearing at my skin like the man in Qom. Who was she, anyway? I remembered what the kids in school had said: "She's really a boy." My body convulsed. Shirin pulled her hands away from me and turned over onto her other side. I opened my eyes and stared at her back, wishing I hadn't moved. She stayed in that position till morning.

After that night, there was an obvious distance between us. Shirin still came over, but every morning, upon rising, I would change my clothes in the bathroom, out of sight from her. In class, I stopped asking her for help, and after school I'd get on the bus without inviting her over. She still came over sometimes, uninvited, to help my mother. Secretly, I was always happy to see her at our front door.

We still shared something, obviously. Something both playful and rebellious. At times, in the school prayer room, we'd giggle and get out of sync with the movements of bowing. I hated the mandatory aspect of praying, but I loved that time with Shirin. To this day, I associate the *azan* (call to prayer) and its heartfelt beauty with getting to take a break from my life, stretch my body, and be next to Shirin.

When we did our *vozoo* (ritual washing) together, I noticed her feet: they were small and a little chubby. I didn't completely understand what I felt, but I knew it had something to do with the feeling that I was sneaking a peak at something exciting. I often found myself staring at the feet of strangers in those days. I think feet have always been a sign of connection for me, even when I was a very young child and saw my mother's feet coming toward me. At those moments, I knew I would be fed and cared for. Feet represented something that I often couldn't get directly.

Most of the students didn't really pray; they just pretended to and whispered gossip to each other between rounds of prostrations. That made me realize I wasn't the only one who hated the compulsory aspect of religion in our school (and every school in Iran). Even Sahar, the most religious girl in my class, who sat on the other side of me from Shirin, was irritated. "This is a show," she'd say. "This isn't Islam. Real Islam is from the heart."

Some of my classmates used prayer time for memorizing formulas on their upcoming tests. They'd raise their hands to their faces in a gesture of reverence to God while whispering, "Samira, in the quadratic equation, is it *b* or *b* squared?" And then, as we'd bow down halfway and say, "Allahu Akbar," Samira would reply, "*B* squared, stupid." I, on the other hand, hated math almost as much as I hated religion, so I spent the time trying to make Shirin laugh instead. I had this trick where I moved my vocal cords with my mouth closed so that my voice sounded like a frog, or maybe a person with indigestion. I'd do this three times in a row, till everyone in the room was shaking with laughter, and our prayer monitor, unable to determine who was playing the prank, would say, "Hell is waiting for you, girls. Don't forget." In spite of laughing at my jokes, Shirin was actually serious about her prayer, and I could tell that, though she was being affectionate with me, she didn't approve of what I was doing.

"Don't pray if you're not going to do it right," she said to me one time after prayer.

"*Namaaz* should not be forced," I said, repeating what I'd heard the old ladies at my mother's Qur'an study group say. "It should come from each person's heart."

"Then why don't you do it from your heart?" Shirin asked.

"Because the prayer is in Arabic," I said. "We are Iranians. I don't speak Arabic. Do you?"

"No," she replied. "But Atash, what if the hell they teach us about is really real?"

"You don't think this isn't hell, what we're living in? People choose what we say and wear, and who we love. I'm sure that when we die, we go someplace better. I have my own prayer that I use when I talk to God."

"What's that?"

"God, if you're listening, please get me out of Iran."

Shirin laughed.

I was kicked out of religion class once for saying that I preferred to talk to God in Persian, my native language. My teacher said I was being disrespectful.

"Islam was brought to us in Arabic. Therefore we must learn Arabic to get closer to God," she informed me as I stormed out of class.

So much didn't make sense to me in those days, but I was certain that if God existed, God could understand me in whatever language I spoke.

I was opening the classroom door to go out into the hall that day when I saw some of the other students nodding their heads approvingly.

"Good job," I heard a few of them mutter.

If people ask me today whether I'm religious, I tell them that I feel guided by something powerful. When I was young, those guides seemed to be inside me, and I still feel that way, though a lot less tormented by what I hear and feel within. It never made sense to me that men should tell a woman what her inner voices were saying. And yet, I do believe in guidance, because when I take time to be still and let a question drop inside my body, clarity always comes. Why would people want to impose their ugly ideas on something so beautiful?

The week after I was kicked out of class, the same teacher gave us a lecture about hell. She talked about how women who showed their hair to men outside their family would be hung by it in hell. They'd be dangled over a gigantic fire by their locks, she explained, till their scalps peeled off, which is when they'd fall in the fire and their sinful bodies would be burnt to ashes. I pictured the kebab seller outside my school who sold roasted meats to students at lunchtime. That thought made me hungry.

"And their cries for help shall be ignored," the teacher went on. "Then, it shall be too late. Hell is for eternity, so after these girls are burnt they will be brought back to life so they can be roasted again and again."

She seemed pleased with herself for having resolved this theological problem. The whole class was quiet. Some looked yellow, as though they were about to faint. But our teacher didn't stop. She was inspired.

"Their fingernails shall be pulled out, one by one."

I gazed around the classroom. Everything was starting to get cloudy. I looked at the teacher, who was still chattering on about Jahannam. She'd become two-dimensional, like a cartoon.

She's funny looking. Her body is round, like a helium balloon. She's a silly, round balloon. Laughable.

Suddenly, I realized I'd stood up behind my desk.

"Hell is for liars who make God look like a vicious torturer," I said, then covered my mouth with my hands, surprised at what I'd done.

"You again, Atash?" the teacher said. "I've had enough of you, Miss Hellfire. You can take your F and leave this class. I won't be passing you." Then, as I followed the now-familiar path to the door, she said, "You were named well, Atash. Fire is what you have waiting for you—"

"God is kind."

I turned around, surprised, and stared at Shirin. She was smiling back at me. The teacher was as startled as I was. Shirin went on in a loud voice, *"Agar oo bireh pas man'am miram.* If she leaves, so do I." The teacher continued to stare. Shirin picked up her things and followed me out the door.

We stood out in the hall, waiting to see what would happen. Then the handle of the door turned. Sahar was standing with us. "Me too," she said.

One by one, the whole class began to come out of the classroom. Pretty soon, we were all standing together.

"I like what you said," one student told me. "She makes God sound like one of the thugs who worked for the shah."

"She's crazy," another said. "Don't worry. She can't fail us all."

A third girl told me that her mother read the Qur'an to her every night. "It doesn't say anything about God torturing children," she said. "Does she think we're stupid?"

I was taken aback, not so much by the rebelliousness of the girls, but rather, by the way they had started talking to me as though I were their friend.

"Let's complain about her to the dean," one girl suggested and led me down the hall, her arm linked in mine.

I'm not sure what happened to our religion teacher, but she never came back to class. No substitute came, either. Only the dean, who told us we should go to the gym and play volleyball. We all had a sense of pride and a new respect for each other. We saw how powerful we could be if we stood together.

When I arrived home that day after we all left class, I found out that the religion teacher had called my mother to discuss my "sinful" behavior. I was sure my mother would find this whole theological discussion laughable, but once again, I failed to predict her behavior.

That afternoon, I found her sitting in the living room, drinking tea, and looking seriously over a copy of the Qur'an.

"Atash-joon," she said. "Do you remember how your father left me when you were born?"

I looked around: the curtains were drawn and the room was much too dark.

"We were so in love," she continued. "There was no way any human could have separated us. It always made me convinced that, at some point, I received a curse." My mother repeated the phrase for "cursed" in Persian a few times, "*Nafrin shodam, nafrin shodam*," bitterly flicking the *f*-sound off her tongue.

"There's a woman who comes to our Qur'an group," my mother continued. "You've seen her. The one with the long nose and bags under her eyes."

I remembered this woman. I had once overheard her telling my mother that a good woman "makes herself available" for her husband "at his wish."

"Anyway, she knows how to free us from this curse," my mother said, her eyes lighting up. "We have to do it, Atash, me and you."

I didn't understand. My mother got up, went into the kitchen, and then came back with her best china plate. I looked in the dish and nearly threw up: it contained a mound of shit.

"Atash-joon, think about it," my mother said. "It's like in math, a negative times a negative gives you a positive. When I was pregnant with you, someone cursed us. We took in something bad, and that bad came through in your birth. Now we need to take in something else bad to cancel out the evil."

"Mommy, what are you talking about? And what . . . whose is that on the plate?"

"Milo's," she said, referring to the German shepherd she'd recently acquired to guard us from the neighbors she thought were spying on us. "And you have to eat it, Atash-joon. Otherwise we'll stay cursed forever."

I told her there was no way in hell I would eat the contents of the plate, but as I said those words, I had a flash of a distant memory—of this having happened before.

Her best china. She did this once before. With her best china.

I realized that my mother was sitting very close to me. Her hand was running through my hair but also gripping it tightly. I saw that look in her eyes that reminded me of no hope.

I started to fight her. Slowly at first, then crazily, as though I were a dog being put down. But my mother was very strong. She started to shriek, "The sooner you get it over with the better!"

I felt my mouth make contact with the warm excrement, and everything went black.

The filth is getting in again. Filth inside these walls, filth inside this door. Think of something. A flower. A pretty girl. Or think of nothing at all.

The next thing I remember, I was lying in my bed. *It's over,* I thought.

But it wasn't over. A day later, my stomach began to churn like a washing machine. Then came a persistent nausea that wouldn't subside. Three days later, my anus began to burn and I couldn't sit still. When I could no longer stand the sensation, I went into the bathroom, squatted over the traditional toilet we had, and ran warm water over my backside. I spent hours in the bathroom, trying to find an escape from the pain in the warm running water.

A week went by, and I started to lose weight. My ribs stuck out, but my stomach was still bloated. Then, one day, in the bathroom, I felt something wriggle between my legs. I looked down and saw the head of a long white worm. I tried to grab its head, but it withdrew into me.

It occurred to me that the beast liked warm water, so for the next few days, I stayed in the bathroom even more. At some point, I felt the wriggling again and saw the worm come out from between my legs.

Grab the snake before it bites you. Grab!

I seized the head of the worm and started to pull, but too quickly—it snapped in half. I stood up and the head dropped into the drain. I pulled the flush cord overhead and half the beast disappeared into the swirling water.

In those days, my father used to drive up to Ramsar every couple of months to see me and my brother. He'd usually get a hotel room and spend the weekend with us there. When he visited next, I told him about the worm and showed him with my hands how long half of it was.

"Worms aren't that long," my father said. "Anyway, they go away."

I was determined to make him believe me, even though I couldn't tell him what my mother had done. *If I bring him the other half, I thought, he'll take me from this place and back to Tehran.* I continued my warm-water regimen throughout the weekend and tried to eat the food at the restaurants he took us to. On the last day of his visit, I defecated, and the other half of the worm came out. I brought my father to the bathroom, and when he saw what was in the toilet, he rushed me to the hospital. There, I was given a massive dose of anti-parasitic medication and confirmation that the beast was real.

But my father didn't take me back to Tehran with him, and he didn't come back to visit for a long time after.

Later, when walking around New York City, I would gag whenever I saw a dog squatting on the pavement. This happened for years. A wave of spasms in my throat would start and sometimes last for minutes. People would ask if I was okay. Of course, no one likes being around dog shit, but it must have seemed strange to others that I would keep gagging for half an hour after seeing it. It seemed strange to me too, because for many years, I had no recollection of what my mother had done to me.

About ten years ago, after I got this particular memory back, I decided to ask my mother about it. We were on a vacation in Turkey, which I had paid for. I wanted, among other things, for her to help me piece together some of my missing memories for this book.

"Mommy-joon, did you think there was something wrong with me as a child?" I asked.

"There was nothing wrong with you, love," my mother replied. "You were a sweet, darling child. You used to get sick sometimes, but you were always an angel."

I felt a burning sensation in my throat rise. There was no backing out now.

"Yes, Mommy," I said. "I would get sick because you would make me sick. Then you would cure me. Then you'd make me sick again."

"Atash, I really don't know what you're talking about. You had worms as a child. I remember that."

"Do you remember why? You said I had evil spirits in me, and you had to cleanse me of them."

"But Atash," my mother said, "look at your life now. You have been cleansed. Your life is perfect. You have love and money. See?"

"Mommy, I had worms because you fed me shit. Dog shit. On your china plates. You don't remember?"

My mom started to gag.

"*Chi migi, dokhtaram*," she said in a low voice. "What are you talking about, my daughter? Shit? Akh, akh. How disgusting. I know you always had an imaginative mind, but dog shit? I hope you don't say these things to other people. You were always a strange, mean child, trying to get your mother in trouble. It was so long ago too. You need to let it go."

As my memories started to return, I remembered how dressed up my mother would get when taking me to the doctor. She'd put on heavy makeup and find her nicest, most colorful scarves to wear, as though she were attending her own birthday party, rather than trying to find the cause of my sickness—which was, of course, her. In my training as a therapist, I learned that this action is called Munchausen syndrome by proxy: a disorder in which a caregiver induces illness in the person she's caring for in order to receive attention herself. If someone had noticed what was happening, there could have been treatment for my mother and me. But there was no such person back then.

A few weeks after my trip to the hospital, a new teacher, Ms. Majidian, took over our high school religion class. She was a younger, big-boned woman with a soft smile and a husky voice. Something about her appearance was a little scary, but when she began teaching, I realized she was much different from our old teacher. Ms. Majidian taught us about Buddhism, Taoism,

Judaism, and Christianity, in addition to Islam. She talked about religions as members of a family.

"You see how one kid has green eyes and another brown, children? But something in each one tells you they're all related. We come from the same thing and return to the same thing."

That was the first day I really felt a part of my school at Ramsar. I actually looked forward to being in religion class. My classmates were friendlier too. In fact, a few of them offered to help me in subjects I was weak in. We were the same. The crazy girl from the big city didn't want to be controlled or threatened by anyone either.

Even though Shirin and a few other classmates were dedicated to helping me, I still wasn't passing any of my classes. What was the point in trying? My heart was set on leaving the country, even if I had no idea how to make my escape.

I bought roadmaps of Turkey and studied them closely. I plotted the points at which crossing the border between Turkey and Iran would be easiest. I didn't really understand what I was studying—I've always been terrible at reading maps—but it was clear that I would have to cross several large mountain ranges. What if I ran out of food? What if I got lost? I'd heard that crossing the mountains was the most efficient way of getting out of the country because Iranian soldiers can't patrol the whole terrain. But that must mean it's hard for refugees too. I needed a guide, someone who was knowledgeable about roads. Where was I going to get the money to pay a guide or find such a person? I watched a few Turkish programs on TV and wrote down the names of a few travel agencies that were advertised. I called those numbers and got a few other numbers. The people I talked to were helpful, but they didn't really understand my situation.

"Why don't you just have your parents buy you an airplane ticket?" one agent asked.

The more I thought about leaving Iran, the more frightened I was that I'd never see Shirin again. And Reza too. I still had a part of me that wanted to discover more with him. I wanted to skip stones together, maybe even kiss him. Shirin brought me letters from him weekly. I was impressed with his dedication in keeping our connection alive. He wrote to me every day from the front. I wrote too but not as much as he did. I really only had bad news to report and didn't know what to write about. I realized that, if we were going to get closer, I'd have to tell him what was going on at home. Finally, in one of my letters, I broke down and wrote that I was probably going to be leaving Iran soon.

"If I don't leave," I wrote. "I'll be married. Either way, there's just no way for us to be together."

I got a letter back from him immediately.

"Please buy time, Atash. Any way you can. I promise I'll be home soon. I'll get you out of this."

I started to think about Reza all the time after that. I imagined him on the Iran-Iraq border, in the midst of battle, finding a quiet corner to write me from. He was fighting for his life and, yet, still finding time to express his feelings toward me. How could I refuse to wait for him?

Shirin loved reading his letters to me over the phone. That was her favorite pastime, especially when she couldn't come over. But often, I could hear my stepfather's breathing over the downstairs phone, so I would often have to change the subject and wait for her to read them to me between classes at school.

One class I loved was poetry. I had several teachers over the years, but when Ms. Majidian came to our school, she started teaching us that class, as well as religion. She always told us, "If people paid attention to words more, they'd also pay more attention to kindness." That really struck me. I could see how thoughtfulness about words was a form of love.

Shirin and I were the best students in that class, and Ms. Majidian often told me that she thought I could be a great writer someday. I had no idea how that would happen, but I was glad that she often let Shirin and I work together.

Once, when we were supposed to be memorizing couplets from Hafez and Rumi, Shirin pulled out a letter from Reza and read it to me. She recited it in a funny, low voice, like a boy's.

"Hello, my love, my fire, my life . . . "—I started laughing uncontrollably to hear those words coming from her mouth— "You must wait for me, my sweet. I'll be there to hold you and caress you."

As Shirin read, she gradually slipped into her own, girlish voice. I preferred that more; it came across as more romantic, more true.

"You are the light that keeps me alive," she said seriously. "You are my hope."

I couldn't remember Reza ever speaking that way. *Maybe the war is softening his heart*, I thought.

My stepfather finally got a big loan from the bank and opened up a clothing store in Ramsar. My mother went to help him. They both seemed happier being out of the house. I, for one, was glad to have a little privacy. Ava, my brother, and I weren't expected to help at the store because we had homework, so our house became a place of freedom. My brother was sixteen now, had no interest in school, and was smoking hash daily. He tried to hide his habit from us, but I, for one, didn't care. When he was high, he was actually nicer. All he wanted to do was to go out with friends and pick up girls, so he wasn't watching our every move.

One day, after my brother had gone out and I was sitting on the couch with my feet up on the coffee table, smoking a cigarette, the phone rang. I got up, annoyed to be disturbed, and answered it.

"It's me. Reza," the voice on the other end of the phone said.

"Reza? *Salaam*," I whispered. I could hardly get any other words out. I was holding onto the kitchen wall.

"I'm a few blocks away," he said. "I have to see you."

"You're here?"

"Yes, just a few houses down."

"I'll be right out. Meet me three houses down from my place, on the right. The curtains will all be drawn, because the owners are in Tehran. But I have to bring my sister with me. I'm watching her right now."

I walked over to the living room mirror and looked at myself in it. I realized Ava was sitting on the couch, staring at me. She was watching me exactly as I used to watch my mother. "Well," I said, smiling over at her. "How do I look?"

"If I help you," she said, clearly understanding everything, even at age seven, "you have to do my homework for me." She meant business.

Fifteen minutes later, I was walking down the street in the turquoise headscarf I'd finally chosen, holding Ava's little hand. The house I had picked for our rendezvous was nearly identical to ours, except that it had a large row of full trees covering it. It was hidden enough to kiss inside but also a short distance from home if we needed a quick escape. I positioned Ava on the front porch where she could watch for my stepfather's car. Then I slipped around the back.

Reza was already sitting on the back porch. He stood up, holding a few gifts wrapped in red paper. He opened his mouth a few times to say something, but each time he seemed unable. Finally, he took one of my hands and placed it on his neck. He was wearing a crocheted hat over his shaved head. It made him look a little girly, but I liked it.

"Atash," he said after a while, "your letters were so beautiful. I read all of them so many times. I can't believe what your family is trying to make you do."

"I know," I said, tears welling up in my eyes. "I was so happy to know you were coming to save me."

He looked at me seriously. "Atash, how could I save you? You know I have to return to the military."

This startled me. "I bought time," I said, "Like you asked me to. I don't know what your plan is—whatever you meant in your letters—I'm sure it will be fine!"

"Atash," he said, leaning in close. "All of my letters to you were returned. I have them all right here." He reached into an inner pocket of his coat and pulled out three envelopes. "You see?" he said, pointing at the little stamped marks on each. "*Bargasht*. Returned."

"Reza, what are you saying?" My voice was getting louder. "You responded to every sentence I wrote in those letters. Don't you remember? 'My love, my fire, my life . . .'"

"Who has been writing you letters?" Reza's eyebrows arched. His body began to tremble in a jealous rage. He grabbed my arms and held me close. "What's his name?" He sounded like my stepfather talking to my mother.

"Atash! Atash!" Ava came running around the side of the house. "Mommy and Baba are coming!"

I grabbed Reza's letters out of his hand and ran with Ava through the backyard. We crossed through several neighbors' gardens till we reached our own back porch. Running into the living room, we sat down on the couch and quickly pretended to be doing homework. My brother was sitting there too, also with a guilty look on his face.

That night, after dinner, I rushed to my room to study the letters I had grabbed from Reza. None of them started with "My love," "My fire," or anything like that. They were all polite but mostly focused on the war and the terrible things he was seeing at the front. In several of them, he brooded over the fact that other letters he'd tried to send had been returned.

The next day I was a mess. All the way to school I kept breaking down and crying. When I got there, Shirin was waiting for me.

"*Salaam*," she said, "What's wrong? You look terrible."

"My parents again," I lied.

"Don't worry, I have good news. I got another letter from Reza for you."

I felt like I had just been thrown into hell, but for some reason I couldn't stop her from continuing her game.

"Yes," I said. "Nothing would make me happier than to hear from him right now."

My situation was becoming very complicated. When I arrived home that afternoon, I got out a notebook and wrote my drama out in the form of a logical argument:

1. *Shirin is the one who's really in love with Atash.*
2. *Atash is the one who's really in love with Reza.*
3. *Reza is really Shirin. At least, she's the one writing his letters to me.*
4. *Therefore, Atash is the one who loves Shirin?*
5. *Also, who is Atash?*

Seeing my name on the page seemed strange. Shirin *was* still my best friend. She was also an accomplice in figuring out how to escape my arranged marriage.

One day, she came up with a plan to get me out of my predicament, once and for all. "Tell your mother in detail about what your stepfather has done," she said. "Once she knows the whole story, she'll have to divorce him. When she's divorced and alone, she'll need you to help her around the house. She won't even think about marrying you off. Bingo! You get rid of your stepfather and your suitors all at once."

"I can't do that," I said. "It will destroy the whole family."

"Reza's heart will break if you don't," Shirin pleaded. "You can't marry someone you don't love."

It was nice to hear her talking about her own heart, even if I knew she was lying about Reza. But I wasn't about to put myself in danger by telling my mother about my stepfather. I knew all too well that she might not take my side. She might even blame me for inflaming his desires. There had to be a better way.

The next day, I went to the beach in Shahsavar, where I had met Reza. I was hoping to find him and understand his real feelings toward me. I walked through the familiar alleyway that took me to our secret spot. I was overjoyed to see him sitting in the sand, wearing the same hat he'd worn the other day. He must have been hoping we'd find each other here too, because he stood up right away with a bright smile on his face and started almost running toward me. He looked so handsome. I walked right into his chest and let him hold me for a long time without speaking. His silent embrace was as strong as mine.

Eventually, he said, "I was going to call your house and ask you to meet me here. But I knew you'd find me on your own."

I looked into his eyes and smiled.

"I'm going back to the front tomorrow, Atash," he said.

"I know."

"What's going on? Who's writing you love letters?"

"It's not another boy," I tried to explain. "It's my friend. She means well. She's just trying to give me hope."

"A girl? Calling you her love, her fire?" He started to laugh.

"What's so funny about that?" I asked. I didn't like that he was laughing at her. "My friend isn't the problem. Don't you understand? My family is. My arranged marriage is the problem. Shirin loves me in a real way."

"What? She writes you love letters pretending to be me and you stand up for her?" He wasn't laughing any more. I could see he was starting to get genuinely jealous. "Well you're going to have to choose between us."

Here we go again, I thought. Another person pulling me apart, just like my parents at the courthouse. But somehow it's never about me or what I want. I wanted to say to Reza, "Fuck off. You can't tell me what to do."

But what I said instead was, "I choose you, Reza! I don't need to think about it at all." And I kissed him passionately, even as I knew I'd never see him again. He knew it too. He was going off to war, and I was going off somewhere else far away. He just wanted me to say the word "choose." And so I gave that to him.

When it was time to go, I took one last, good look at him. Tears were running down his face. He stood and watched me walk away but didn't follow or call after me. Every time I looked back, his image was a little smaller.

That night, I invited Shirin over to study. When she arrived and I saw the enthusiastic expression on her face, I asked my mom to excuse us early from dinner. I told her that we had a lot of math homework to catch up on. Shirin looked nervous. Perhaps she knew I had found out about the letters. I could feel her close to me as she followed me to my room. As soon as we were inside, I locked the door. I stood there watching as tears formed in her eyes.

"Are you okay?" she asked.

"I know about the letters," I said as I took off my T-shirt, then bra.

I could hear how heavily she was breathing. She sat on my bed, watching me undress bit by bit, until I was only in my underwear.

"Your parents . . . ?"

"Shh. Don't talk. We're studying."

This was the first time I really had sex. I knew I'd never forget that day. I got to choose each move: where, how. This was the first time *I* was having sex. I told Shirin to keep on some of her clothes. I got on top of her and put my breasts in her mouth. She grabbed them timidly, then roughly, as she sucked on my nipples. I whispered in her ear that I loved her. I watched her mouth move slowly, the veins of her neck pulsating as I rubbed myself on her body and pubic bone.

"Do you?" I asked.

"Do I what?"

"Do you love me?"

"You really have to ask?

"Tell me then" I said.

"It doesn't matter, Atash. This is Iran. We can't be together. Besides, you are going to leave."

Her voice was defeated, but her body kept grinding against me until it happened, and we both collapsed on each other, overwhelmed by the pleasure we'd found.

It was hard to fall asleep next to her that night. She was right. I'd never heard of girls being together. I took comfort in the fact that my first orgasm with another person was with her, but I also kept thinking about Reza. I didn't want to choose between the people I loved. Why couldn't I love them both? There were, in fact, many things I loved about both of them. I loved the fact that Reza could cry. I'd never seen a man cry before. And I loved Shirin's poetic way: her soft voice, her love letters. What's wrong with being with both of them? What if I could find a way?

These days, it's easy to say that I identify as queer. But even calling queerness an identity, let alone embracing it, was impossible back then. My feelings seemed like a tragic mistake or failure of design, but I couldn't figure out what I'd done wrong, or where this all had started. As with so many aspects of life, I chalked my queerness up to my mother's belief that I was a jinx. It actually made sense: to love someone of each gender and end up with neither of them, wasn't that the ultimate curse?

14

SCARLET

I'm Scarlet. I'm young and fearless. The others think I'm reckless, but I know I'll always find the things I need along the way.

I don't trust men. With all the beautiful women in the world, why would anyone choose a man as a lover? I like making men want me, but more than that, I like using them to get to women. When I attract a man, I learn all about the women around him: their deepest fears and desires, what makes them feel alive, what makes them feel dead inside. The others think I cause trouble, but this is my story, so I'm going to tell it my way.

Down by the sea, a few kilometers from the House, there's a beach where the Ivory Armies do their riding practice every day at dawn. The girls in the House like to sit up on the dunes and watch the handsome knights ride past, gossiping about who is the most charming. I used to sit on a bluff, a few yards from them, and look to see if any of them would notice me. One did. He was young, not very handsome, and short, but graceful in the way he moved. Everything he did seemed perfectly timed. That's why I thought it was strange when, as he galloped by, he dropped a leather satchel in the sand.

I picked up the satchel. It contained about fifty sealed envelopes, addressed to various inhabitants of the Far Island. I didn't know what that was, and despite my curiosity, I realized there was no way for me to open the sealed letters without being caught. I decided to return the satchel and see if I could learn more about this mysterious knight that way. I knew that there was a garrison half a mile down the beach, so I walked in that direction until I came to a group of stables. I knocked on the door of one of the stables, and a woman dressed in men's riding clothes opened the door. I gathered she was the girl paid to look after the knights' horses. She was handsome, and my stomach felt funny when I spoke to her.

"One of the knights dropped this bag," I said. "The short one. Do you know who I mean?"

She made a laughing movement with her face, but no sound came out of her throat.

"You can't speak?" I asked.

She nodded. And then she did something I wasn't expecting. She reached out and touched a few strands of my hair that had fallen forward and smoothed them back. Then her hand fell limp at her side.

I wanted her to touch me like that again.

"I don't mind if we can't talk," I told her. "There's a place near my house where the landscape is so beautiful that everyone who goes there forgets how to speak. Maybe we could go together some time?"

She smiled again. I noticed her teeth were very bad, but there was something about her face that made it impossible for me to turn away.

"I live in a house made of stone," I continued. It's hidden inside the mountain just over the dunes there." I pointed with my hand. "Come find me." Then I said goodbye and left.

I never saw the stable girl again — at least not in the same form she was that day. Some of the other girls in the House said that she tried to find me once. I was angry with them for preventing her, but I had no idea what she'd become in the hands of Green.

One day, there was a knock on the door of our House. We're not allowed to open the door to strangers, so I sat motionless for a while, but finally, curiosity got the better of me and I peeped through the keyhole.

I blinked. The stable girl seemed to stand before me, holding a bouquet of wildflowers! Overjoyed, I unlocked the door and embraced her. She pressed her body to mine and kissed me full on the mouth. Her arms were muscular, and I held them tightly. We kissed again, this time with open lips. I felt her tongue explore my mouth, and something cold and wet slid between my lips. I leapt back, confused, with a snake writhing between my teeth. I tried to pull it out, but the slimy thing pushed itself deeper into my body and settled in my belly. I could feel it moving around inside me.

"What have you done!" I yelled at the stable girl, but she was no longer the stable girl. To my horror, it was the Witch standing before me. She laughed a hideous laugh.

"You stupid girl," the Witch said. "I own you now."

"Where is the stable girl?" I stammered.

"She was always an illusion," the Witch said cruelly. "All your dreams are illusions. I'm the only real thing here."

I turned and ran. The Witch chased me through the kitchen and out the back door of the House. I ran through the garden with her close on my heels, but the path kept getting narrower, and at some point, I had no choice but to run through the bushes and thorns. My dress tore as I charged through a large rose bush. The Witch followed, but suddenly I heard her scream. I looked back and saw that the rose bush had grabbed her with its spikes and imprisoned her with its branches. It spoke to me: "Run, my love. You belong in a better place. I wish you all the happiness in the world." I paused for a moment, then kept running.

That night, in the cover of darkness, I came back to the House to see what had happened. I found the other girls gathered by the White Pool.

"The Witch is here!" I cried. "She found our location."

"We know," the others said. "Our bags are packed. We're leaving for the Far Island."

15

ROCK BOTTOM

In the summer before my senior year of high school, my father moved to a bigger place in Tehran. After years of making excuses for not being able to have me live with him, he suddenly informed me that I could stay with him through August. Life in Tehran felt exciting but also lonelier. I didn't have Shirin or Reza or anyone I knew to spend time with. Seeking some sort of distraction, I got involved in political activism. This gave me a new life.

It was the late 1980s, and many of the grand ideals of the Iranian Revolution had become reduced to petty issues—mostly involving how women dressed and acted. In those days, female officers belonging to the Komiteh, or morals police, would patrol the streets looking for girls wearing lipstick. One time I was walking down the street in Tehran with a girlfriend named Neda, an activist I'd met on the bus one day. She worked for a woman's organization that was secretly distributing feminist pamphlets in schools. I remember their program was pretty modest: she was trying to encourage women not to get married too young, to form bonds with other female intellectuals, and to have some self-respect.

As Neda was telling me about her work, a white Paykan car with two men in the front and two fat women in black chadors in the back pulled up to the curb. The two women got out and began to walk toward us. I could see they had rifles slung around their shoulders. Neda began to shake. She whispered to me, "Atash, I'm carrying a lot of pamphlets right now in my backpack. I'm going to put it on the ground. You have to pick it up and take it to Ekbatan."

The two women with guns surrounded us and began to yell at Neda, "Shame on you!" I assumed they knew about her political activity, so I tried to distract them by focusing their attention on me.

"We didn't do anything," I said.

"Your lips!" one of the fat women shrieked, pointing at Neda. "How did they get so red? From eating pomegranates? That's lipstick she's wearing!" I realized the women had no idea about the pamphlets in the backpack.

"I'm not wearing lipstick," I protested. I wasn't. All of a sudden a hand went up and clocked me in the face.

"Shut up!" the fat woman screamed. She went over to Neda, pulled out a large wad of cotton, and thrust it at her. "Clean your lips!" she shouted. Both women started pointing their guns at Neda. Neda began to scrub her lips furiously with the wad of cotton, and the two women turned around and left. I was shocked to see them leave so abruptly, but when I looked over, I saw there was blood all over Neda's face.

"You're bleeding all over!" I screamed. She looked down at the wad of cotton the women had given her.

"They put broken glass in it," she said. Tears ran down her face, making clean streaks through the blood.

"I probably need stitches for this," she said, between fingers dripping with red. "I'm going to call my brother and have him take me to the hospital. But I still need your help. Will you do it?"

"Of course, Neda," I said. "Whatever you need. Just ask."

"Take this backpack and deliver it to the address on this piece of paper. It's a house. There are lots of nice women there. You should know them." She took a pen from her purse and wrote down the address. I couldn't take my eyes off of the torn flesh of her lips. She was so calm, in spite of being disfigured.

"Neda, are you going to be alright?"

"Here is some money," she said. "Take a taxi." She thrust a few tomans into my hand and turned to leave.

"My family knows a good plastic surgeon," she said. "Atash, make sure you deliver the backpack."

People still underestimate the extent to which control of female sexuality was and still is at the heart of what keeps the Islamic Republic going. Boys still learn that their "honor" comes from how well they can assert dominance over a woman. Since 1979, when the government first created Islamic youth camps and leagues, young men have been taught to find self-esteem in pacifying and disciplining their wives, daughters, and sisters. And some women are taught to police female sexuality in an attempt to find an identity and protection for themselves. If this dynamic comes to an end, no one will continue to support a government that has otherwise done nothing for its people, economy, and society.

People forget that Mahsa Amini, the twenty-two-year-old Kurdish woman killed at the hands of the Iranian morality police in 2022, was actually wearing a hijab. Yet in the wake of protests following her death, the president took the opportunity to pass an order further expanding hijab laws to include social media, so that now anyone caught without a headscarf on their profile pictures could be arrested. He was saying, in no uncertain terms, that Mahsa's death wasn't about police brutality but about women being responsible for the violence of men. The Islamic Republic's message to women has always been: if you make men feel something they can't control, we will disfigure you.

Neda was right. The women I met at Ekbatan inspired me. They had the same light in their eyes as the revolutionaries from my father's generation. That summer, Neda's family sent her away to Turkey, and I took her place in the ranks, helping the women carry their pamphlets from place to place. They liked how I looked; one of them told me I had an "innocent face."

The first twenty or so deliveries I did for them went smoothly. Then one day they asked me to go to a high-rise apartment complex in the middle of Tehran. I had to enter through a central courtyard, which was covered with beautiful trees and flowers, and give a codename to the guard there. He let me in with no problems, but as I rode the elevator to the twelfth floor, I realized my stomach was doing somersaults. This has always been a bad omen for me.

Inside the apartment, there was a smell of tea in the air. There were twenty women sitting on couches around a coffee table piled high with nuts and sweets. They were passionately discussing the topic of divorce. When I walked in, a few of them got up to greet me, but the rest didn't pause their conversation.

"Please stay for the meeting, Atash," one of them said. But I didn't feel like staying. I felt sure something bad was about to happen. I quickly drank the tea they had given me and headed for the door, leaving the backpack with them in a corner of the room.

As soon as I got outside, I saw a few pickup trucks parked in the street: the kind the Komiteh always drove. Two men got out from the back and called me over.

"Where's your backpack?"

"I don't have a backpack," I said.

"No, you had a backpack," one of the men insisted. "What did you do with it? Where did you drop it?" He stared at me. "You're in a lot of trouble. Tell me what you're doing here."

My heart dropped when he said that because I realized I hadn't prepared an alibi. What was I doing here? Then it came to me. My brother knew a girl named Atusa who lived in the same complex and was a hairdresser. I told the Komiteh I was trying to find her apartment.

"What's her last name?" one of the officers asked.

"I'm not sure," I said. "She cuts hair. That's all I know. I wanted to get a perm."

They didn't believe me. They took me down to the station, where I stayed overnight in a damp cell with no bed and only one wooden chair. All night long, I heard the voice of another woman in a nearby cell screaming in pain. I never managed to make out why she was there, or what they were doing to her, but my imagination kept me in perpetual fear until morning.

The next day, I was interviewed by a senior Komiteh member: a tall, skinny man with greasy hair and a big beard. He looked as though he hadn't taken a shower in a long time. I realized that he didn't care about my story. He was only interested in seeing how much money he could get from my family. He threatened me with fifty-six lashes, clearly hoping I'd put extra pressure on my father to bring lots of cash to the station. But I couldn't call my father. What if he refused to bail me out? What if he sent me back to live with my mother? The fear of being rejected kept me from calling. Then I remembered that a boy I'd known in Ramsar had a father who worked in the government. I told the Komiteh official his name.

"This man is practically part of my family," I said authoritatively. "Call him and say Atash is here. I'll be happy to tell him what you've done to me."

I hadn't expected this ploy to work, but the official got really, really nervous. He had clearly heard of my friend's father.

"I see," he said. "Well, there's really no need to talk about it, then." And he let me go.

As a social worker, I understand how important these kinds of personal connections are. I've seen myself able to get kids out of serious trouble by knowing the lawyer or the housing official. It makes me happy to be able to do this, but every time I succeed in pulling strings, I often think of all the people who don't have those connections. In Iran, the Komiteh might come for rich people, but they're only looking for a bribe. If you're poor, "morality" means something else: being arrested or even shot and killed.

That fall, when I went back to Ramsar to live with my mother and stepfather, my mother told me that she had heard about my run-in with the Komiteh. Some friend of mine, flirting with my brother, had told him about that day, and he had promptly reported it to my mother. The conclusion she drew from this incident was that, by remaining unmarried, I was drifting into the dangerous clutches of feminism. Yet for some reason she didn't bring up the issue of marrying my cousin right then, though I knew it was still on the table. For a few weeks, I was free to focus on my studies.

But then, one night at dinner, I felt heavy stares, not just from my stepfather—who always stared at me—but from her too, and I knew exactly what was coming. After the meal, I quickly washed the dishes and ran to my room. I remember I was reading a book about a woman who fled her country and her abusive husband. Within minutes, my mother stormed into my room, forcing me to put down my book.

"I've been thinking," she said. "Your wedding to Shahpour will be in the spring. We don't even have to wait till graduation. Spring is such a perfect time for such a perfect union."

"I'm not marrying my cousin, Mommy."

"But don't you see, Atash? Family is the way. Family doesn't care about your problems. Family will accept you just the way you are."

"Is something wrong with me?" I asked.

"Well, your aunt knows about your hygiene issues and your old peeing problem. She's not even worried that you get 'possessed' sometimes," my mother said brightly. She rolled her eyes back in her head to illustrate this point.

"Mommy, please leave me alone. Please let me focus on my studies."

"No one else will want you, honey," she said, trying to look sympathetic. "This is the best solution. Besides, Shahpour has always loved you. Who will you find that's better than him?"

"Mommy! I don't want to marry *anyone*."

"Please think about it."

Disgusted, I said, "Okay, I'll think about it. Now let me finish my book." I had no intention of giving her proposal another thought.

"This world of fantasy will bring you nothing but disappointment," my mother cautioned me. She switched off the light as she went out.

"Mom!" I yelled. "The lights!" She came back in, turned the light on, and sat down next to me on the bed. She started to cry.

"Please don't cry," I said. "I promised you I'd think about it."

"What is it you really want from life, honey?" my mother asked in a sweet voice. I could tell she was using her good cop/bad cop routine to butter me up.

"I have no idea," I said. "I'm seventeen. Why would I know that?"

"Well, you must have an idea or a dream of some sort."

"Okay," I said. "I want to go to a different country, learn to speak a new language, get an education in that language, get a job, rent my own apartment, have new friends from all over the world . . . "

I couldn't stop talking. I went on describing what my apartment would look like, where my friends would all be from. Then I stopped short when I saw my mother's face change color. I didn't know if she was about to scream, laugh, or cry.

"What's wrong?"

"Give me that book," she demanded. "This garbage is polluting your mind."

I was furious. "Take it! I don't need it anyway! My life will be better than any damn book. You'll see!"

The next night, I didn't join my family at the dinner table. I wasn't hungry. I stayed in my room and got lost in my running-away fantasies. I had a bad headache too. Ava came in and asked me to tell her about the book I was reading at the time: the memoirs of Napoleon's wife. But she didn't seem to be listening as I summarized it for her. At one point, she closed my book.

"What is it with you?" I asked her.

"Everyone thinks you've lost your mind," she told me.

"Is that what they say?"

"Yes. Where are all these new clothes coming from?"

Act surprised.

"Which ones?" I asked.

"The ones that you put away last night when you thought I was sleeping."

I had no idea what she was talking about.

Yes, you do. The clothes you're storing up for when you leave this place.

"They're from my father," I lied.

"You haven't seen your father since the summer," Ava observed. "These were brand-new clothes." It always amazed me how Ava, despite being ten, saw things so clearly. Then she said, "Everyone thinks Sepehr likes you because he's coming around so much lately. Do you like him?"

"Sepehr?" I asked, only half hearing her words. "That's crazy talk." Sepehr was a friend of my brother. His family owned a farm. I had no interest in milking cows for the rest of my life.

"Let's go to sleep," I told her. "I'm too tired for this nonsense."

I tossed and turned that night. My mind kept me up wondering what kind of new clothes I had put away. When I was sure Ava was asleep, I got up and went over to the small closet in the corner of our room. There, I found two luxurious, brightly colored scarves, a long tunic, a few new T-shirts, and a very pretty red dress. This dress was very strange. I hated wearing dresses, and the fancy scarves weren't at all my style. The T-shirts made a little more sense—I used to wear them under my school uniform—and the tunic, though I never would have picked it out, seemed pretty. But I couldn't remember buying or receiving any of them.

I went back to bed but couldn't sleep. My mind kept trying to solve this puzzle. I believed Ava when she said she had seen me putting the clothes away, but I couldn't remember anything else. Did I buy them myself? Why would I do that? I got up, turned the light back on, and started looking for receipts. Nothing! Then an idea occurred to me: I'd count all the money I had saved to see if any had been spent. I used to keep my allowance in two locations: one in the bottom of my closet under a rug and a few empty suitcases; the other inside the mattress on Ava's bed. I checked the bottom of my closet first. The envelope that had held my money was gone. There was no need to look further. I must have bought those things.

I told you what the clothes are for. We're going to be prepared for what happens next.

I looked to see if I had written any notes about Sepehr. I found a whole entry about him in my journal. It said that Sepehr's sister was a vet and that he worked with her. Apparently, I was fascinated by his stories of horses and cows giving birth, and cats and dogs surviving surgeries. These notes also contained a date when I was supposed to visit him at the vet and meet all the animals. I was stunned. I had absolutely no desire to see this boy, and I couldn't remember ever having made plans with him.

September 30th. That's what we said. Don't forget the date.

I felt like an old, senile lady. I wondered if there was such a thing as Alzheimer's for young people.

I decided to open up to Shirin about what was happening to me. "Do you think I'm possessed by an evil spirit?" I asked her. She laughed.

"Who do you think I am, your mother?"

"I'm serious, Shirin. Brand-new clothes are appearing in my closet. And strange words are scribbled in my notebook. Yesterday, I found a whole page with things on it that said, 'Please remember this happened.' 'Please don't trust Mommy when she is sweet.' 'Please remember to hide your money from your brother.'"

"Atash, I think those kinds of things too. I just don't write them down."

"But each paragraph is in a different handwriting, Shirin."

I got out my notebook and showed her.

"Yeah, that's kind of weird," she admitted. "Sometimes I do have to explain things to you a couple of different times. Maybe your memory doesn't work so well, but I don't think that has anything to do with magic. Maybe you need to eat more carrots."

The way she was speaking made me feel safer. I decided to say more.

"You know, Shirin, when I'm staring off into space, it's not nothingness. There's somewhere I go. It's a house made of stone, and it's very beautiful. I don't know if it's another realm or just a part of my brain. But I know it's not bad."

"Like a fantasy world? Of course we all have that."

"Maybe it is," I said, feeling defeated. But as I said it, a sadness welled up in me. "No, it's not fantasy," I said, changing my mind. "It can't be. It's me."

"Atash, let's not talk about this anymore. You're just giving your mother more excuses to be horrible to you."

The rest of my senior year went on fairly quietly. I hung out with Shirin a lot and tried to stay out of any trouble that would speed up the marriage process. As spring came, I was relieved to know that I'd be spending the summer again in Tehran after graduation.

My final exams didn't go well at all, however. In history class, I found myself coming into consciousness only after the test had come and gone. Apparently, I'd disappeared into myself for the whole hour I was taking the test. I don't remember much about my math exam, except for the end, when I came back into my body to find the teacher shaking me and yelling, "Atash! My God! Her face is all blue!"

I couldn't breathe.

You're going under. There's nothing you can do to stop the sinking. But you can still breathe, even when you think you can't.

The next thing that I saw was a hospital room. There were lots of people crowding around my bed, but I didn't recognize any of them. The hours were all a blur.

It's hard for people who aren't trauma survivors to understand what it's like to be in a constant state of panic. Everyone has experienced shocks, but it's hard for most people to imagine what it's like to lose track of time on a regular basis. Sometimes when I work with kids who have survived war, I see the relief in their faces or hear their sighs when I tell them this lost time is normal. It makes me happy to see but also a little sad too. I really wish someone had told me that when I was their age, so I wouldn't have had to feel so sick and broken.

The next day, I found myself sitting on the couch with my mother. She had given me some cigarettes (apparently she knew I'd been stealing hers for some time) and we were smoking together. She told me that she had been one of the people in the hospital room with me, but I hadn't recognized her. The doctors told her that I had collapsed during an exam and was brought to the hospital because I appeared to have amnesia. They wanted me to be placed in the custody of a psychiatrist, but my mother intervened.

"I told them they are the ones who need psychiatric help," she told me proudly. And then, changing in her characteristic way, she added, "I didn't want them to find out about your evil spirits, Atash. You should thank me for that."

I wanted to tell her to go to hell, but I felt terrified. What if she was right about the spirits? I knew I wasn't evil, though. Could I be possessed by good spirits?

I wanted to ask her if this was possible, but suddenly her head fell in a gesture of despair.

"How can I give you away without a diploma?" she moaned.

"Mommy, I'm graduating in a few weeks."

"Atash," she said. "You failed all your classes. Every single one."

Part of me was relieved to hear this. Not graduating meant postponing the wedding even longer. But part of me knew my condition was getting worse. I felt very out of control.

I convinced my mother to let me go to Tehran for the summer anyway. Apparently, the school administration had said that, because I had a medical excuse, I could retake my exams in August and, assuming I passed them, could graduate in September. My father promised to hire a few tutors to work with me over the summer, which he never did, though my youngest uncle stepped in to work with me.

That summer, my father said I should stay with his mother, Maman Moneer, since he had already promised to house my brother, and my brother and I were fighting all the time. I didn't object. In fact, I was looking forward to living under Maman's roof because she didn't place so many restrictions on me. I had unlimited access to her phone and, unlike my stepfather, she had no interest in eavesdropping on my conversations.

My mother called me frequently that summer. She was keen on making sure nothing interfered with her plans for my wedding, which she insisted I keep a secret from my father and Maman.

"That old witch will ruin your marriage, the same way she ruined mine," my mother warned me.

Nevertheless, my mother seemed happy that I was in Tehran. I think she thought that with Shahpour and me in closer proximity to each other, the two of us would hang out and somehow fall in love. Shahpour's mother, whom I called Khaleh (Aunt), lived near my grandmother's house. Khaleh was pleased that I was in town. She talked about my wedding to her son as though it were a fact and frequently asked if I'd like to go shopping with her "for supplies"—meaning things I might wear to the altar. She'd already started to call me *dokhtaram*, "my daughter." Having had two sons, she always wanted a daughter and treated me like her own. I loved her too, and part of me didn't want to disappoint her.

Shortly after I settled into my grandmother's place, Khaleh took me out for lunch. As she was paying the check, she said, "Atash-joon, I'd really like to take you to look at some wedding gowns. You'd have to be fitted in person, so this might be our only chance."

For some reason—either out of exhaustion or out of wanting this kind woman to take care of me—I said yes.

At the first bridal shop, a saleswoman greeted us who looked as though she could have been my age. Unlike me, she was thrilled about our search for the perfect dress and talked as though marriage was the best thing that could happen to a girl.

"I am going to help you try on every dress we have here," she informed me.

"Exactly how many are you talking about?" I asked. She made it sound like we were about to scale the tallest peak in the Alborz Mountains.

"At least three hundred."

Even my poor aunt seemed disturbed by this number. The girl didn't give us time to think, however. She led us directly to where she kept her favorite dresses.

"I'll help you put them on," she told me. Then she whispered in my ear, "Or do you want your mother to help you?"

"She's not my mother. She's the mother of the groom."

The girl looked at my aunt and smiled suspiciously. Then she pointed to a couch and asked Khaleh to sit down.

"You can wait for the bride here," she said. "She'll be appearing from those doors over there."

As soon as the girl and I entered the dressing room, her smile dissolved. "Take off your clothes and put on this one first," she barked, thrusting at my face a long, poofy dress with frills all over the sides.

I held the dress in front of me, waiting for her to leave, but she didn't, so I started to disrobe. The girl just kept standing there, her head turned to one side, watching my reflection in the mirror.

"I can see all your bones," she said, staring at my ribs. It was true. I was very skinny in those days.

"How old are you?" the salesgirl asked.

"Seventeen," I said.

"You look fourteen," she remarked. Then she thought for a moment and asked, "If you're seventeen, why aren't you excited about your wedding?"

It occurred to me that this girl was anxious about not making a sale. I said nothing and continued putting on the stupid dress.

"I'm twenty-four," the girl went on as she zipped me up. "I can't wait to get married. So I can get out of my father's house."

I studied myself in the mirror. The gown was radiant, and I couldn't believe how beautiful it looked on me. I started to cry. *This is it*, I thought. *I'm getting dressed for hell. At least I look pretty.*

The girl studied my tears. "Are you going to buy it or not?" she said.

"Yes," I said. "I'll take this one."

Khaleh bought the dress for me and held on to it for safe-keeping. Then she dropped me off at Maman's place. I felt really bad for her. I knew I was going to disappoint her.

"Atash," she said. "I know your mother isn't well. I know it's been hard living with her. I really hope I can take care of you now and life can be easier."

When she said that, I wanted to die. *If I could only die*, I thought, *all of this would just go away.* But part of me still wanted to run.

And then I remembered my mother's words: "Don't say anything to Maman Moneer—she'll ruin your wedding."

And a plan started to form.

When I got back from shopping, I found Maman Moneer in the kitchen, frying eggplants for *khoresht-e bademjoon*, the stew she was preparing for dinner. This dish was my father's favorite, and she was preparing it because he was coming to visit. I stood in the doorway and, without even saying hello, said casually, "I'm getting married in less than a month."

"Married?" Maman kept careful watch over her eggplants. "To whom?" she asked, as though I'd been recounting the plot of a movie to her.

"Shahpour."

"And how come I didn't hear about this?" Maman said, still showing no sign of emotion.

"Because my mother thinks you'll sabotage the wedding," I said, watching her eyes roam over the pot in front of her. She flipped the eggplants from the fried side to the other.

"Your mother won't invite me to my granddaughter's wedding?" Her top lip curled over the bottom one in annoyance.

"Maman-joon," I cried impatiently. "Your being invited or not isn't the point!" I couldn't believe she had nothing else to say. "I'm getting *married*! The wedding is in a month, and my jewelry and dress are picked. It's real."

Maman stopped her frying and looked at me carefully. She took my hands in hers and walked me to the living room. "We have to tell you father tonight," she said. "Tell me first, do you *really* want to marry him?"

"I don't know. It's just . . . " I was sobbing by this point and couldn't finish my sentence.

"I see," Maman said. "Say no more. I'll take care of it."

Then her face changed. "My eggplants!" she cried and rushed to the kitchen. From the other room I heard her yell, "You aren't even done with high school! What's the rush?"

But I was still anxious about delivering the news to my father. What if he got angry that I would even be considering marriage before my graduation and never want to see me again? Or, what if he secretly felt I was a burden and wanted to use the wedding to get rid of me? The truth was: I didn't know my father and was scared of finding out his real feelings toward me.

Maman evidently picked up on my anxiety, because she sent me down to my uncle Afshin's apartment (he lived right below her in those days) and told me to wait while she talked to my father herself. I used the time at Afshin's place to write a letter to Shirin, but even that didn't pass the time. After what seemed like an eternity, my grandmother called and told me to come back up. When I rang the bell to her apartment, my father opened the door.

"Well, well," he said. "Look at my flower."

He had a smile on his face, but I knew he only used that sort of pet name when something was bothering him. My stepmother Afsaneh came to the door and kissed me hello. My brother and my little half sisters Setareh and Samira, five and eight years old now, were all there too. I greeted everyone. Maman's husband, Baba Bozorg, was sitting in an armchair near the door. I studied him particularly, as he was famous for not being able to keep a secret. People used to say that when he played cards, you could see his whole hand just by looking at his face. Two shot glasses filled with vodka smuggled from Turkey were balanced on the arm of the chair next to him, and it wasn't even dinner time yet. I tried to keep my cool and walked into the kitchen.

"Can I help with anything Maman?" I asked.

"Yes, set these plates on the table," Maman Moneer said, without looking at me.

Dinner, usually a noisy affair, passed in relative silence. After the food had been cleared, I got up to use the bathroom. I realized, however, that my legs felt strangely numb. With difficulty, I walked to the bathroom and sat down to pee. As I was pulling up my jeans, I had the sensation that my legs didn't belong to me.

They don't belong to you. You're going under. There's nothing that can stop the sinking.

My legs gave way, as though their bones had withered, and I fell down on the bathroom floor. I was confused but pulled myself up and walked out into the living room, supporting myself with the walls. Now my hands started to feel numb too. The only part of me that seemed to work was my torso. I made it halfway into the room and fell down again on the floor.

"Atash!" Afsaneh yelled. "What's wrong?"

"I can't walk," I said.

My dad and brother rushed over to me and pulled me up to stand. As soon as they loosened their hold on me, I dropped to the floor again. Once more, they pulled me up. I felt like a baby fawn learning to walk.

"Okay," my father said. "You're okay." But I wasn't. He let go and I fell again.

I could hear my brother saying, "Strange things have been happening to her lately. She keeps collapsing."

Just when I was getting used to lying down on the floor, a new sensation hit me. I felt something pull from within my spine. I thought my neck was going to break, it was so painful. It was as though something or someone were pulling my head backward to touch my back. *I am possessed*, I thought. *Just like in those horror movies on TV.* I tried to straighten my body, but I couldn't. I was having a hard time getting air into my lungs.

My father started to yell at my brother. "What's wrong with her? What's wrong with her?" he repeated. I felt my grandmother's hands on my face. And then, all of a sudden, I felt my whole body lift up into the air.

You see how free you are? You can leave and travel wherever you like. I'll show you how.

Then I passed out.

When I came to, I was in the backseat of my father's Renault. Our whole family was piled in too. Afsaneh kept asking my brother, "What do you mean this keeps happening to her? For how long?" I couldn't see clearly, but I gathered we were on our way to the hospital.

We entered the triage room, and doctors started coming from all sides. They had needles. I kept yelling, "My neck is coming off!" I heard one doctor say he'd never seen anything like this. The shots kept coming and, eventually, I relaxed, but my neck still seemed disjoined from my spine. It was a while before I fell asleep.

Now rest. The plan is coming together. You just need to let it happen.

I haven't experienced anything quite that dramatic in a long time, but just the other month, I was in a four-day professional training with other therapists who didn't know me. At some point, we were asked to do simple drawings, and as I drew, I lost track of time. Later on, the drawings were posted, and another teacher came up and said that she loved mine. "You're so connected to your inner child," she said.

I found my drawing and saw, to my embarrassment, that it looked as though it had been done by a four-year old. The drawing had little suns and moons, and the structure in it looked exactly like the House of Stone.

As soon as I saw the picture, I felt a twisting in my neck start to happen, as though someone were tightening screws on it. By the next day, my shoulders were completely glued to my ears and everything hurt when I walked. Because it was Sunday, I went to the emergency room, where the doctors injected me with a muscle relaxer. It was a good reminder that my past is never that far from me.

That night in Tehran, I woke up in my father's house. It was night, and I was in my sister Samira's bed. Light from an outside streetlamp shone into the room, and I saw the stuffed bears and dogs that my uncle Amin had made for Samira. He had made some for me too. Through the crack in the bottom of the bedroom door, I saw people walking back and forth. *They must be so worried about me*, I thought. Here I was, in this happy little room filled with toys and books and all sorts of kid's things, and I felt totally out of place.

That was the first time it occurred to me that I didn't want to be there anymore.

Not just in my father's house. Anywhere at all.

I sat up with support from my hands and realized how little energy I had. The streetlamp was throwing different patterns on the window curtain. I crawled over and looked out. I was hoping to catch sight of some people passing by—coming home from their parties or dinners—but there was no one, just a lot of concrete. I could almost feel how hard the concrete would be, waiting there down below. My head was pounding, and I felt as though the only thing that would make it go away was a collision with the ground.

Think about how many people you won't be able to disappoint once you're gone, I thought. I pictured my mother, father, Khaleh, Shahpour, and everyone else carrying little framed pictures of me.

"She was such a good girl," they were all saying in my mind, pointing at the face in their photographs.

I opened the window.

There was a breeze blowing on my face and on the curtain. I had a surge of energy. I felt like the wind. I looked down at the concrete three floors below and leaned my body toward its embrace.

Fall. Let yourself fall.

But I didn't fall.

Instead, I felt a strong, rough hand on my foot. In an instant, a great force jerked me back into the room. My father stood above me, the skin on his face stretched tight as a drum. His wide eyes were fixed on me, pure fire. I was sure he was going to kill me. I instinctively pushed my thumbs into my eyeballs, as I had done when I was little.

Fly like a bird over Vali Asr. Fly, fly over the whole city. Disappear.

But I didn't disappear. I started to cry. My breath got shorter and shorter, till I was using my whole body just to find the tiniest bit of oxygen.

Suddenly I felt the entire width of my father's hand come down on my face. Bang! Then on the other side of my face. Bang! Everything stood still, and I realized I wasn't breathing at all.

Then I heard Afsaneh's voice yell, "Stop! Stop hitting her! She's been through enough!"

"She was trying to kill herself! You want me to stop?"

But he did stop, and he got down on the floor next to me and started to sob.

Maman Moneer stayed with me for three days and nursed me back to health. After the third day, my father came into the room with my grandmother and sat down on the edge of my bed.

He gave me a glass of water and said, "I need to know what's going on with this marriage of yours."

"My mother will be disappointed if I don't marry Shahpour."

"Do you want to?" he asked me. The skin on his face wasn't stretched any more. It was loose and pulled down over his face, as though gravity had increased.

I was afraid to say the word. Whenever I tried to form it on my lips, I pictured my mother crying, the way she had after my father had left her. *This is the man who betrayed my mother*, I thought. Now I'm about to help him do it again.

"Atash-joon, this can't happen," my father said sternly. "You're much too young to get married." I stared at him. My throat started to loosen. "Listen," he said, rubbing his hands together nervously. "This is what we're going to do. I'm going to invite your aunt and Shahpour here, so they'll have to ask me in person for your hand in marriage. After all, I'm your father. They can't skip that important step."

I didn't say anything. I was happy that my father was on my side, but he didn't understand my situation at all. Even if I got away from this marriage, how would I get away from me?

Two days later, when I was feeling better, my aunt, her husband, and Shahpour came to visit. Maman Moneer made me exchange my T-shirt for a festive striped dress. Afsaneh saw to it that I had a bit of lipstick on. Then the two of them sent me into the living room. I saw my father sitting next to one of his old friends, Akbar, whom I hadn't seen for a long time. I gathered that Akbar was there to play the role of mediator. Shahpour was sitting on the couch to the left of them; my aunt and her husband sat on their right. Maman Moneer was strategically sitting between Khaleh and her son. As soon as they saw me walk in, everyone got up to greet me.

"The most beautiful bride!" my aunt called out as I came in.

I sat down next to my aunt as she asked me to, my face turning red. Then it occurred to me, rather strangely, that everyone in the room appeared to be having a good time. They were talking about food (always a favorite topic in my family), and my grandmother offered the guests fresh fruits, nuts, and sweets. Afsaneh seemed especially attentive to me, helping me bring out the tea and offer it to everyone. Shahpour sat across from me, smiling kindly. He had a gentle presence.

"We are so happy to have you involved with the wedding," my aunt said to my father.

"I'm glad to be part of it," my father said diplomatically, "but usually there is no wedding until the father agrees." He smiled at my aunt. "Isn't that right?"

Khaleh tried to change the subject. "Didn't Atash-joon tell you about the dress we bought for her?" She looked around the room as if to say: this is a done deal.

"No, she hasn't," my father said severely. "I thought you had all come here today to talk with me about this marriage. I have no objections, but I must say, I am disappointed to hear this talk of dresses before being consulted."

"We're sorry, Baba Khan," Khaleh said. Adding *Khan* (Sir) showed she was being respectful but also that she was losing ground. "We *hope* we have your blessings."

"I'm an old lady," Maman chimed in, "But if I may, I have a question, too."

The whole room fell silent.

"Who could be better than Shahpour to marry my granddaughter?" she began. My aunt looked happy, but it was clear that Maman hadn't asked her question yet. The whole room held its breath. "I'm wondering where Atash is going to live after the wedding?" Maman went on. "Does Shahpour have enough money to pay for an apartment, a car, and bills?"

Shahpour's parents winced, but Shahpour replied confidently, "I'm in college right now, Maman, but when I finish my studies, I intend to get a well-paying job and buy my own place."

"When will you graduate?" my father asked. It was clear to me now what was happening.

"In two years."

"Wait, let me understand this," my father said. "So for two years, where is Atash going to live while she's your wife?"

Khaleh leaned forward in her seat and said, "What did *you* have when you married my sister?" She looked around, but it was clear no one was going to help her answer the question. "Nothing," she said to herself. "You were just a scrawny nineteen-year old."

And then she crossed a line.

"We gave you our little sister," she continued, mumbling now. "And you left her with two kids."

Something awful had been unleashed in the room, like a poison gas. I watched as it started to distort everyone's faces. Khaleh felt its effects too and started to cry.

Here it comes. Watch.

But my father, surprisingly, looked as though he'd been waiting all night for those exact words. He said, without blinking, "You're absolutely right, Khaleh. I made the biggest mistake of my life when I married her. That's exactly my point."

Khaleh was flustered. "The point is—" she said. "The point is that these two kids love each other, and we adults have to give them support." She looked around the room, as if searching for the support she was talking about.

Maman Moneer, calculating the exact midpoint between Khaleh's position and my father's, said, "I think the point is that rushing into marriage will bring problems for everyone."

Now my aunt's husband spoke. "This will be different," he said, "because the couple will live with us for two years and we'll take care of them until they're ready to be on their own."

This was all news to me. My father looked at me like a lawyer skillfully cross-examining his own witness. "Did *you* know, Atash-joon," he said, "that when you get married, you will be living with your aunt and uncle?"

I shook my head no. So this is what they meant by "taking care of it." I was impressed by my father's checkmate. But I was also alarmed by what I was hearing. *So my mother knows that the person I'm supposed to marry isn't even going to be there*, I thought, *and I have to live with his parents for two years? Everyone just keeps passing me around.*

"Atash, tell your father you want to marry my son," my aunt said. Tears were streaming down her face. Seeing her cry made me feel even more frustrated. I started to cry too.

That's okay. Keep crying. Just don't try to stop what's happening.

"It's okay, Mom," Shahpour jumped in. "I can wait for Atash till I grad—"

But Shahpour's father cut him off with a hissing sound and got up to leave. "This is a total mess," he said, looking at my father. "I can't believe I agreed to come here in the first place. For one thing, I can see why Atash's mother didn't want to take you back."

"Don't say that!" my aunt shrieked at her husband. "Please, let's stay and talk this through." But he took her arm and dragged her out of our house.

"I am sorry, Khaleh-joon," I said, running after them.

My aunt turned and gave me a sad smile. "I really tried to help you, Atash. I don't know what else to do to get you out of your mother's house."

Then she left.

The last to go was Shahpour himself. "I meant what I said," he told me. "I'll wait as long as you like." I studied his face. He was a kind, caring gentleman after all.

"Merci," I said, and closed the door gently.

Looking back, I feel gratitude to my aunt for trying to help me survive the only way she knew how. Later, when I worked as a counselor in a high school, I learned how important it is for teenagers to know they can count on adults for help—even when the teenagers are rebelling or pretending to be independent. My aunt wanted to be the one who would take away my burden. But she, like all the adults in my life then, never asked what my burden was, or what I wanted, for that matter. Maybe I didn't know what I wanted. Maybe what I needed most was time to figure that out.

My mother didn't call me anymore that summer. I settled into life at my grandmother's house and began to actually enjoy the summer. My uncle Amin—my grandmother's youngest son—was technically still living with her, though he was usually out partying or camping with his friends. He was in his late twenties by now, designing machines that produced dolls and puppets. I got along with him more than the rest of my father's side of the family. Amin tutored me in all my subjects and was easy to be with. He couldn't understand why I was having so much trouble passing my exams. He saw that I could explain what I learned back to him very well. But whenever he said, "Okay, Atash-joon, today we're going to have a short exam," something changed and I couldn't answer a single question correctly.

"When I asked you the same questions a few days ago, you answered every one perfectly," he'd say, perplexed. "Why not now?"

I definitely wasn't going to tell *him* about the House of Stone.

In late August, my brother and I went back to our mother's house together. This was the first time we'd seen her and my stepfather since my father had sabotaged the wedding. They came out of the house shouting at both of us right away. My mother grabbed hold of my hair and my stepfather shook my brother, whom they had somehow also implicated in this heinous plot against them.

"You've betrayed us!" my mother shrieked. "This is the biggest embarrassment in the whole history of our family. All those guests who were supposed to come! What are we going to say to them?"

"Tell them the bride and groom decided to postpone the wedding till he finishes university," my brother suggested, trying to get one foot in the front door. I noted that this was one of the first times in years that he was actually trying to help me. My stepfather held him fast, though.

"There will *never* be another wedding," my stepfather said savagely. "Your aunt won't even talk to your mother now."

"How did I raise you two to become my enemies?" my mother wailed.

The ordeal was over, though, and there was nothing more to be done. My brother and I went inside and immediately started to relax. It was clear that my mother just had to vent.

That month, I began to suffer long bouts of insomnia. Something strange was still happening inside me. At two in the morning, I'd find myself unable to sleep and consumed with the thought that I had no idea what I'd done that day. I dug around my room, like a detective looking for clues, with even more persistence than before. I found the same notebooks filled with notes about people, all in different kinds of handwriting, but this time I also found a map of Turkey that someone (me, I'd guessed) had annotated with the words: "Staying here is the same as dying, but leaving is the same as suicide. Which will it be?" I looked at it and recoiled in horror.

Eventually, I fell asleep that night. The next day, I woke up with a splitting headache. I was disoriented, and it was hard for me to do the simplest tasks, such as getting my clothes on, gathering my books. It seemed like two boxers were duking it out in the ring of my head. I heard my stepfather say that today was the day of my makeup exams and he was taking me to school himself to make sure I went.

As soon as I heard him go to the bathroom, I slipped out the back door and walked as fast as I could to the bus stop. I was determined to get to the exams on time and without him souring my mood. But that day, everything seemed to be happening backward. All the city people from Tehran were packing their bags to leave their summer homes, just as I was heading to school. On the bus, I lost track of time and had to backtrack two stops on foot to get to my school. Walking in the streets, I saw empty houses and cars leaving town. My head was throbbing.

Can you hear it? The sound of the ocean in a seashell? Take it all in.

I looked around and realized I wasn't even close to my school. There was sand all around, and I recognized the familiar beach in the secret place I met with Reza. Had I come there to meet him? I couldn't remember. There was a burning sensation in my belly and an awful taste in my mouth. I felt so ill. I looked at my watch and saw that it was eleven. Two hours had passed since my exam had started. I looked up and saw seagulls flying low in the sky, noisily fighting each other for scraps of leftover fish. I felt the fabric of my long, black chador on my body and pulled it around me. For the first time in my life I appreciated that piece of clothing. "Chador" means "tent" in Farsi. I imagined myself like a camper in the wilderness, hidden away from the dangers of human civilization.

I looked down and noticed a plastic bag with a bottle in it at my feet. I took out the bottle and saw that it was half filled with bleach. I held it to my nose and the smell confirmed for me that I had drunk it. The pungent smell matched the taste in my mouth perfectly. Without giving it another thought, I opened the lid, covered my nose, and took another sip. The burning in my stomach rekindled. I became even more dizzy than I already was. I tried to stand up, but I couldn't. My clothes felt so heavy. *I'm wearing too much*, I thought. I'm going to explode.

I started crawling toward the sea. She was calling me. I needed to cool off. I kept crawling, crawling, like a little child, till the first waves hit my face. I felt the tide lift me up. Now I was swimming. The sea pulled my clothes from me. I let go of the hem of my chador and watched it whirl down to the bottom. I let go of my hair covering too.

You're free. You're finally free.

The cold of the water on my skin met the heat beneath it, and I felt my core start to relax. *I won't drown*, I thought. *I know how to swim. I won't drown because I don't want to die.* But the sea had taken my clothes and was clawing at my skin.

It wants you. It wants all of you.

Then everything went dark.

When I opened my eyes, I found myself in a steamy room. Hot water seemed to be running on all sides of me. There were two beautiful women: one middle-aged, and the other young, like me. They were washing my body. The two women were clothed but soaking wet, taking turns supporting and cleaning me.

"She's awake," the younger one said.

"Am I dead?" I asked.

"You're lucky," the older one said.

"The fisherman found you drowning," the younger one said. "They brought you to the first house that opened its doors."

"Can you hold yourself up?" the older one asked.

"Were you trying to drown yourself?" the younger one asked.

"Not now," said the older one. "Later."

"Where are my clothes?" I asked. I realized I was naked except for my underwear.

"I'm washing them," the older lady said. "You threw up everywhere. You can wear Negin's for now," she said, pointing to the younger girl.

I got up slowly. There was still the awful smell of bleach everywhere. I saw that I'd thrown up all over their shower room, but the smell of bleach still overpowered everything.

I put on Negin's clothes, walked slowly out into the hall, and found the first mirror I could. The reflection in it seemed like that of an old woman: the eyes were sunken into the head, and there were dark circles spreading into the cheeks; the skin was white, and there was blue on the lips. Had years gone by? Had I woken up old? I saw what looked like a dining room off to one side and walked into it. The older lady was now sitting at the table.

"Salaam," I said and sat down next to her.

"My name is Mrs. Noory," she said. "I'm Negin's mother. What's your name?"

I couldn't remember, and that scared me. I said nothing.

Negin came in. "What were you doing in the water?" she asked.

"I don't know."

"Sweetie," Mrs. Noory said. "We need to know who we can call, so we can let them know you're here."

"There's no one to call," I said. It was the truth. I couldn't imagine anyone in the world at that moment who could have been connected with me.

"So you don't remember anything?" Negin asked.

"Okay, okay," Mrs. Noory said. "Please eat something now. You're going to be okay."

"How long can I stay here?" I asked. I was hoping she'd say forever.

"As long as it takes for us to find your family."

A few days passed. I remember there being a big library in the house and getting lost in the stories I found there. It seemed possible to me that I'd never leave. But gradually the pleasant atmosphere of the house began to wear off. Mrs. Noory's face started to lose its smile, and she no longer let me wander around the house, but, rather, she followed me with probing eyes. *I need to make it up to them somehow*, I thought. One evening, I found a pile of dirty dishes in the kitchen sink and started washing them. Mrs. Noory came into the kitchen with Negin. They seemed upset.

"You still haven't told us your name," Mrs. Noory said.

"I . . . I can't remember," I said, even though I did. I didn't want her to call my family.

"Your name is Atash, isn't it?" Negin asked. She looked at me intensely.

"What is it that you're not telling us?" Mrs. Noory said. Then, "Were you trying to kill yourself?"

"No," I said. "At least, I don't think so."

I finished the dishes and sat down with them on the couch. Finally, I asked, "How do you know my name is Atash?"

"I went through your backpack and saw your school ID," Negin said. She gave it back to me. "We found it on the beach."

"I contacted your school and got your mother's phone number," Mrs. Noory said. Then she looked down at me from over the rim of her glasses and asked, "Atash-joon, is there anything you want to tell us *before* your parents get here?"

"My parents?" The idea seemed impossible.

Then the house bell rang a few times in a row.

"That must be them," Mrs. Noory said.

A woman and two men came through the door. The woman was crying loudly.

"I thought my daughter was dead," she said. "How much can a mother take?"

Mrs. Noory invited them into the living room where four couches made a semicircle. I was afraid to look up at anyone. Mrs. Noory sat next to me and stroked my back.

"You can tell us what's wrong, and we'll all put our heads together to help you," she said. She looked at her guests for confirmation. "Isn't that right?"

"We don't know what to do with Atash anymore," the woman said, not answering Mrs. Noory's question. "Every week it's a new problem."

"Problem?" Mrs. Noory asked.

"She acts strange at home and in school. Her friends don't even know her anymore. She recently got herself out of a perfect opportunity for a good marriage."

"The problem seems to be that she tried to kill herself," Mrs. Noory said. Then she faced me and asked, "What do you think, Atash?"

"She just wants to play around," one of the men said. "We have a name in this town, you know. She's ruining it for us."

"Can we please hear from Atash?" Mrs. Noory seemed impatient with her guests.

I felt all eyes on me. I looked up and studied the three people in the room: the crying woman, the angry man, and the third who sat quietly on one end of the sofa. He in particular drew me in. I studied his face and then, all of the sudden, it hit me: Sepehr! My brother's friend Sepehr, the one who works with animals.

"We're all here for you," Mrs. Noory said as she kept rubbing my back. "We just want to find a way to help you, Atash. You've been such a delight since you got here. You're so kind and thoughtful. But you cry a lot—before you sleep, when you wake up."

I didn't remember crying, but I felt myself start to now. "I don't know," I sobbed. "I can't recall anything. Each morning I wake up to a brand-new day, not remembering anything about the day before. All I know is something really bad is happening and my mind keeps hiding it from me."

The strange woman leaned forward in her seat and passed some papers to Mrs. Noory.

"Here are the love letters she's been writing to Sepehr," the woman said. "She just got out of a perfect opportunity to marry her cousin, and now we know why."

"She writes like Rumi but can't pass any of her exams," the angry man said.

"Please wait a second, ma'am," Mrs. Noory said. "This is what I do for a living. I work with many girls who struggle with memory loss. After a few days with Atash, I can tell you that this is an emotional issue, not a cognitive one."

Then she turned to me. "How long have you been forgetting things, Atash?"

"I'm not sure. Since I've been very little, it's always been this way."

I looked around the room and rubbed my eyes. I kept blinking until the angry man's face came into focus. My stepfather. Then I looked at the woman and realized she had to be my mother. I blinked again. My mother. It didn't seem possible, but there she was.

Mrs. Noory passed me the stack of letters. I read a few of them. They were in my handwriting, but I couldn't remember writing any of them. I felt as though someone had published my personal bank code in a newspaper for all the world to see.

"Atash-joon," my mother said. "Tell us what you want. Do you love Sepehr?"

Of course not, I thought. I must have just been killing time by writing to someone who gave me attention. But what could I say? I had no idea what I'd written, and all those letters in my handwriting were lying right there in the palm of my hand. I started to rock back and forth. My fingers reached up to my head and I started kneading at the flesh of my scalp. Slowly, I started to tug at my hair, pulling at it harder and harder. Mrs. Noory got up, alarmed, and grabbed me in her arms. She held me to her, and I started to weep uncontrollably.

"See?" my mother said. "See? This is what she does."

At Mrs. Noory's insistence, my family took me to the nearest hospital in Shahsavar for X-rays of my esophagus and stomach. Mrs. Noory demanded that she ride along. I was very grateful for her presence. The X-rays came back okay: apparently I had thrown everything up before it could do any serious internal damage. But the doctors wouldn't release me, despite the protests of my mother and stepfather. One of them, a psychiatrist named Dr. Kazemi, an old man with a long nose, glasses, and a bald head, insisted on taking me into a side room for further questioning. He had a funny Rashti accent that made him sound like he had marbles in his mouth.

"Atash-*khanom*," Dr. Kazemi said when we were alone. "You're very lucky to have met Mrs. Noory. She's one of our best therapists."

"You know Mrs. Noory?" I asked.

"Of course," he said. "She works here at the hospital. She told me a little bit about your forgetfulness. I wanted to ask you a few questions, if that's okay."

I didn't say anything.

"I want to make it clear, Atash, that I am not going to discuss what you say here with anyone else."

For some reason, I felt I could trust him. But I didn't know where to begin, so I just said, "It didn't start as forgetfulness. It started as losing track of time. Sometimes I'd just be pretending I was flying or traveling to fun places. And then, somehow, I stopped being able to tell what was real."

Dr. Kazemi peered down his narrow nose at me. "You sound like a clever girl, Atash. Maybe you can tell me what was happening when you used to imagine flying?"

You don't have to talk to him. He seems nice, but you don't know.

I went on, cautiously.

"I remember doing that when my grandmother used to tie us to the bed, so she could go out shopping and not have to worry about us."

"For how long did she tie you to the bed?"

Okay, you can tell him that.

"A couple of hours, sometimes all day," I said. "It was okay then . . . but I think my forgetfulness got worse during the revolution."

Dr. Kazemi seemed to understand. He nodded his head several times vigorously. But then there was a silence between us, and he didn't break it.

"Dr. Kazemi," I said after a few minutes. "Do you want me to tell you why I was trying to kill myself?" The words sounded like someone else's coming out of my mouth.

"Yes," he said. "That's the question I've had in my mind."

Stop! It's a trick. He's getting information for the Witch.

"Are you really a safe person?" I asked. "Or will you hurt me like the others?"

"My job is to help you, Atash, not to hurt you. And I think I understand what's happening, but I need you to tell me a bit more."

I took a deep breath, and everything started to come out.

"I'm not a virgin," I said. "I haven't been since I was little."

He nodded patiently but didn't say anything.

"When I close my eyes," I said, "I often see bad things happening to me. But they can't all be real. There are too many of them, and they're too horrible. Sometimes I press my eyeballs to stop seeing that and I end up in a different realm. Does that make sense?"

I put my thumbs in my eye sockets to show him. I thought I heard him say something, but then I felt myself being pulled to the House of Stone. I struggled against the hands pulling me, and the room got bright again.

"You're back," Dr. Kazemi observed. I saw he was smiling.

"Why are you smiling?" I asked.

"I like your sense of humor. Do you know what we were just talking about? How long do you think you've been in my office?"

I didn't know what we were talking about, and I was shocked when he said I'd been there for almost two hours.

"Atash," he said, finally. "Do you know why people forget things?"

His question struck me as strange. I didn't know why.

"People forget things in order to survive. If we remembered every terrible thing that happened to us, we wouldn't be able to bear it. So you see, your forgetting is very brave. It's your mind protecting you, like a loyal dog that won't let anything hurt its owner."

"But Dr. Kazemi, I can't control when it happens. It's not something I choose. I mean . . . Do you think I have Alzheimer's?"

Dr. Kazemi laughed. "No, Atash. I don't think you have Alzheimer's."

I was encouraged by this. "So you're going to treat me, then? You're going to give me medicine?"

"I'm afraid there's no medicine for trauma, Atash," he said. "But time is the best medicine of all. You must come see me regularly for therapy, however. I've treated many people with your condition before. How does that sound to you?"

You see? He doesn't understand your situation at all. He's like the others.

I felt a hot flush of anger in my cheeks. "How can I go to therapy, Dr. Kazemi? My parents already think I'm crazy. They're going to treat me worse than they already do. And what do you mean, my 'condition'?"

"I believe you have multiple personalities," he said. "I've already met two or three different parts of you today, and they're all wonderful. But I need more time to help you understand how to work with them."

His words stung. *Multiple personalities.* I remembered one of our neighbors, Mrs. Yekta, who was very old but still sometimes dressed in colorful teenage clothes. My mother had warned me to stay away from her. "Chand shaksiyatiye divoone," my mother whispered under her breath. "She's many people. She's insane."

"So you are saying I'm crazy, Dr. Kazemi."

"No, I'm saying you're profoundly hurt. Therapy is for healthy people who are wounded, Atash. And I will tell you honestly: if you don't get help, you might try to kill yourself again."

But I couldn't take in any more. *Multiple personalities.* Was he insulting me? I had nothing more to say to him. Anyway,

I wasn't scared of dying. I said goodbye and found my mother and stepfather in the waiting room.

But as soon as I got home, I realized I wanted to see Dr. Kazemi again. I asked my mother if I could, but she said, "There's something wrong with that man, Atash. I could see it in his eyes. He's just another crazy person with a degree."

A few weeks later, I was sent back to live with Maman Moneer again. I think my mother knew that if I stayed in her house, I'd succeed in killing myself.

My uncle Amin went back to homeschooling me. I was too ashamed to sit in the same grade one more year in Ramsar, so my father had arranged for me to finish high school in Tehran. One evening, while I was being tutored, Maman Moneer interrupted us.

"Your mother is on the line," she said. "She says it's important."

I walked over to the phone and picked it up. "Hello?"

"Salaam, Atash-joon."

"Salaam, Mommy-joon," I said. "Is everything all right?"

"Yes," she said. There was a pause at the end of the line. Then she said, "Atash-joon, do you still dream of leaving Iran?"

"Is something wrong?" I asked. I didn't understand where she was going with this.

"Atash-joon," she repeated, "If you still want to leave, listen to me. One of my distant cousins has a son who lives in New York. His name is Ali. He was just rejected by his fiancée who says she won't leave Iran to be with him. There's going to be a party in Tehran in a month, and Ali's mother will be there. Atash-joon, we can go together and meet her. They're still mourning his previous engagement. They'll be so happy to know it can work out with you."

I didn't know anything about Ali or his mother. But I didn't care. On the other side of the world was New York, the only place I could imagine staying alive. I remembered a photo I'd seen in one of my uncle's smuggled *Time* magazines of a woman in yellow pants and a man in an orange shirt coming out of a fancy hotel, grinning ear to ear. I'd cut out the photo and taped it to the first page of my notebook. There are happy people in this world, I thought. It's just Iran that's all dark.

My mother seemed to read my mind, because she said in a low voice, "I'd rather lose you to another country than to death, Atash. Besides, you can make it up to me by sending me money."

"Yes, Mommy," I said. "I'll meet Ali's mother."

16

BURGUNDY

I'm Burgundy. For years, I've worked as a servant in the House of Stone. The others leave me their dishes to wash, silver to polish, furniture to fix. They don't appreciate how much I do for them, but I take comfort in the fact that, as long as I'm working, I don't have to feel the enormous sadness inside me. The others think I'm slow, but that's just because I'm careful. I won't do things without a plan. They're always running from here to there, but I wait patiently for an opening.

The day the Witch chased Scarlet around the garden, the others were ready to leave the House of Stone right away for the Far Island, but how were they planning to get there? The Witch sees all the creatures in the forest, and her owl armies would pick us off right away. I'm no fool. Besides, there was something heavy in me that day. I still don't know what exactly, but I felt as though my feet were like concrete blocks. I wanted to be alone. With effort, I walked down to the White Pool, where I could be alone to think.

At the edge of the White Pool, I was surprised to see a rowboat. I didn't remember one being there before. Maybe it washed up from downstream? Anyway, I had the idea of rowing out to the center of the pool and sitting there for a while, so I picked up the splintery oars and rowed out beyond the earshot of the other girls. In the middle of the water, I felt a deep sense of calm come over me. I thought I heard someone whispering, "I wish you could join me," but I looked and saw no one there. *Maybe it's my own voice*, I thought, *or else the sound of the willow trees brushing against the water.*

All of a sudden, I felt my eyes fill with tears. I can't explain exactly what I was thinking about, but I started to cry. It was a gentle trickle of water at first, but soon I heard myself sobbing, and the flow increased. I looked down at the bottom of the rowboat: my tears had started to form a puddle. I began to wail louder and the puddle got deeper. I thought to myself that I should pull myself together, but I couldn't stop crying. The puddle rose to my ankles, then to my knees. The heaviness inside me got stronger. I looked and saw that the water from the pool was starting to enter the boat, mingling with my tears. *I'm sinking*, I thought.

The boat went under. I tried to break free and swim, but my legs were too heavy. I saw the world on land disappear and the world beneath the water welcome me. My hair trailed above me like a flag. "Is this how I'm going to die?" I thought.

But for some reason, I was breathing.

I can breathe underwater, I said to myself.

Rainbow-colored fish swam by me, stared for a moment, and then passed on. Turtles gave me a knowing look. The seaweed embraced me. The watery kingdom was enormous.

Then there was a thud, and everything went black for a moment. When I regained my vision, I was pinned to the ocean floor. Something was holding my body down—it was the weight of the boat—and only my head and neck were free. I twisted and turned, and found, to my surprise, that my neck and head were elastic and were free to explore the underwater world as far as I desired. My head roamed the sea floor, beholding submarine caves, sturgeon, eagle rays, and coral reefs. I felt exhilarated and, for a moment, forgot about the weight of my trapped body.

Gradually, I became aware of faces on the bottom of the sea floor. As my head moved closer, I saw that the faces were human, soft and gentle, but belonged to large oysters, whose shells were rough and sparkling. I became aware that the Oyster People were talking to one another. They were trading terribly sad stories about how they'd come to live on the ocean floor: one had been an opium addict and lost his whole family and inheritance; another had been in a car accident that killed her newborn son. The Oyster People listened to each other's stories with compassion, pausing after each one, then continuing with a new tale of woe. At some point, I heard one say, "Lady in the Rowboat, why are you here?"

"Tears sank my boat," I said, realizing how ridiculous that sounded.

"That happens," another said. "But make sure you want to be here. The longer you stay, the harder your shell will become."

"You all seem very happy," I said. "You listen to each other and understand, not like the people I live with above water. Besides, your shells seem like good protection from future danger."

"We have no future," the Oyster People said. "We've been dead for centuries. Our shells keep our souls from scattering, but everything else you see in our faces is long gone."

"Am I long gone too?" I asked.

"Not if you still have something left to give the world," they said.

"What do I have to give?" I asked.

But no one answered. The underwater world seemed very still and dead. All of a sudden, I realized I didn't want to be there. A bit of feeling returned to my arms and legs, and I saw that, if I tried, I could push myself out from under the boat that had pinned me. As I started to struggle, I heard a small voice.

"Will you at least take a gift from us before you go?"

I turned and saw the smallest of the Oyster People—a little girl of about eight—holding a basket with her mouth. In it were a thousand tiny pearls, each one a slightly different color and size.

"Are you sure?" I asked her. "There are so many."

"More than you can count," the Oyster Girl said. "It will take you a long time to spend them all. Go on, now."

I wriggled my body and felt it detach from the rowboat. I turned the boat over and sat in it. Then I took the basket from the Oyster Girl and the boat began to rise. As I ascended, I turned back to wave goodbye to the Oyster People, but they all had their faces pulled back inside their shells. The light above grew more intense, and I heard the voices of my sisters crying out to save me.

17

FROM RUGS TO RICHES

For a long time, part of me blamed myself for breaking my mother's heart. In my guiltiest moments, I believed I was a curse who had separated her from two men, rattled every nerve in her body by setting myself on fire or drowning myself.

My brother, one year out from his own high school graduation, finally had to do his military service. He'd been putting it off, but the government came for him. Through my father's connections, he got a service position, far from the war front, in Tehran, which for him was a dream come true. My brother wasn't exactly the soldier type, with his skinny body and hashish-smoking ways. He was happy to be assigned as a "bodyguard" for some ayatollah, which meant, in theory, that he was supposed to take the bullet for the cleric if he was attacked or assaulted but in practice meant passing time in a brand-new Range Rover, smoking joints, hitting on girls, and generally forgetting to pick the holy man up from his meetings with important theologians.

At my grandmother's house, Uncle Amin continued home-schooling me through the fall. He was a genius in math and physics and spent his free time building machines that built small toys for children. He kept these in his bedroom where we had our sessions and gave me illustrations of scientific concepts not just through words and pictures, but physically, with the apparatuses he had scattered around his room.

My mother called me in November to let me know she was coming to Tehran from Ramsar. I met her at the Hilton, where she'd booked a room for seven days. "We're going to see each other a lot this week," she said. She was giggling like a teenager at a slumber party.

"Atash-joon," she said when we got to her hotel room, "I want you to look your best tonight. This is your ticket out."

I didn't respond. I had a vague memory of what she was saying but couldn't place it.

"Tonight is Ali's mother's party," my mother went on. "It's in Farmanieh." She paused. "Where rich people live. Atash-joon, I have a really good intuition about this."

She was talking to me differently now, as though I were her best friend, someone whose interests she had at heart. *Maybe I can make it up to her*, I thought. *I'll marry Ali and send her lots of money from America.*

Her hotel room had huge windows that looked out over Vali Asr Street and its tall trees. It was strange to be looking out on the same street where I used to imagine flying like a bird.

"Thank you for helping me, Mommy-joon," I said.

"Thank me later. Now show me the dress you said you brought to wear."

I didn't remember bringing a dress, but I looked in my bag and saw I had brought one. My mother didn't like it. "It makes you look like a little girl," she observed. "You already look younger than your age. We need to make you look like a woman."

"I'm eighteen, Mommy-joon. I am a woman."

My mother seemed unimpressed. She took the dress from me and tossed it on the bed. "I don't want them to think they have to raise you," she said. "They should see a wife, a future mother in you."

We left the hotel room and got into an elevator with a group of women with nose-job bandages, highlighted hair, silk scarves, and far too much makeup on. I'd never been in such a lavish place before. Outside, my mother walked me down Vali Asr in search of the perfect dress. I realized that this was the first time my mother had ever taken me shopping for something fancy. She was so patient as she watched me try on successive dresses, and I felt an immense pride when she finally settled on an outfit for me: a dark green, tight-fitting dress that revealed every inch of my body. I felt uncomfortable about wearing it in front of so many strangers, but it did make me look really pretty. Maybe this dress will make me brave, I thought. But then it occurred to me that I didn't want my shopping time with my mother to be over yet.

"Can we look around more?" I asked.

"You don't like it?" my mother asked in surprise.

"I do," I said. "Why don't you think I do?"

"Because you're crying," she said.

I wish I could have said to her then what I know now: *Of course I was crying, Mommy-joon. You were watching out for me and thinking of my best interest. You were being a mother to me, at last.*

In the cab to the party, my mother's kind demeanor started to fade. "Atash," she said, gripping my arm, "You can't afford to pull any of your crazy stunts tonight. You can't get, you know . . . possessed."

I promised her I wouldn't, though I had no idea how to keep that from happening.

The taxi dropped us off on a dead-end street, and I saw lots of expensive parked cars.

"Are all these cars coming for the party?" I asked.

"Everyone is here to show off their girls," my mother said. "But don't worry. No one can compete with mine." She clearly took this competition personally.

But I *was* worried. I thought: *My life changes from black-and-white to color and back again in a flash. Like Dorothy in* The Wizard of Oz.

The doorman ushered us in, and traditional Persian music trickled out from the house. We walked into the most enormous courtyard I'd ever seen. Well-dressed people stood around holding cups of tea. There was a little fountain at the center where, my mother informed me in a whisper, members of Ali's immediate family were standing. One of the people by the fountain—Ali's mother, I gathered—saw us and came running over. She embraced my mother for a few moments, then looked me up and down.

"Atash!" she exclaimed. "I almost didn't recognize you. All grown up! The last time we met you were nine." I couldn't remember having met her, but I smiled in agreement.

"And then," Ali's mother said excitedly, continuing the conversation she'd obviously been secretly having with my mother," . . . and then, the best part of the ceremony will be when all the unmarried girls dance a traditional Bandari chain dance together." I had no idea what she was talking about, or how to dance that way. "And I hope you can participate, Atash," she said with a smile.

"She would be delighted to," my mother said.

My mind started to flicker.

All these people look like Disney cartoons. The old men in suits are puffed up like balloons. Thick makeup is melting down the faces of the eager debutantes. People's voices are high and funny. And you, my dear Cinderella, can do whatever you want now. Nothing is real.

My mind started to steady itself. I noticed that the people around me looked real again. But now, I was wearing a scarf around my hips that was shimmering with woven coins. I also saw that I held a candle in each of my hands. I was dancing now, moving my shoulders and hips. I was dancing with fire.

People started applauding, and when I looked to see why, I realized I was leading a ring of beautiful girls behind me.

You are the leader. The others worship you.

The dance ended and all the mothers clapped again. "You're great," someone said to me as I walked over to the edge of the room and sat down. I was still trying to figure out what had happened in the time that had escaped. My mother was anxious. She knew I'd been "possessed," but this time my possession seemed to be working in my favor. I felt a massive headache coming on.

In a matter of moments, Ali's mother was by my side again. She took my hands in hers and led me from the crowd. "Atash," she said, "Where did you learn to dance like that?"

"I don't know how to dance," I said. It was true.

"Humility!" she exclaimed. "What a wonderful quality for a bride to have."

She walked me to her bedroom and showed me a picture of Ali. "Your mother said you wanted to see my son's picture," she said. "Well, what do you think?"

"He's handsome," I said. It wasn't such a lie. He was balding a little, but in the photograph he had a nice smile and was lying on a beach wearing shorts. He looked, at the very least, like someone who knew how to have fun.

"So you like my son?" Ali's mother said. "That's wonderful. But tell me, how do you feel about leaving Iran? Could you manage to leave your family behind?"

I suppressed a giggle. "Yes, ma'am," I said. "Leaving here will not be a problem."

But Ali's mother was still anxious. "The girl who was behind you in the ceremony is the same girl who was supposed to marry Ali," she said. "Two days before her flight, she called to announce she couldn't leave her family. Girls have such a hard time separating from their mothers, I know. I just don't want to have to spend all that money again for nothing."

I looked at the photo again. Ali was older than I'd imagined. No, definitely not handsome, I concluded. But then there was his smile again. I really liked that smile.

"I can tell you will be good for him," Ali's mother said. "There's something about your eyes that don't lie."

I thought this over but didn't respond.

"And don't worry about the age difference," she said. "My husband is ten years older than me too. It's actually perfect like that."

Ali's mother and mine sealed the deal that day. The only problem was, again, that my mother had made a plan for me without consulting my father. On the way home, I reminded her that he needed to be told what was happening. My motivations weren't totally unselfish: I needed him to be part of the plan in case my mother turned on me at the last moment, as she often did, perhaps finding me a local suitor who would promise her more money.

I told my mother I'd talk to my father myself and win him over. Surprisingly, he liked the idea of me marrying Ali right away.

"You have my blessings, Atash," he said. "But tell me, what's the rush? You're still so young, and this engagement seems to be happening so fast."

"I just know I have to get out of Iran," I said.

"I can understand that," he said. "Things aren't good here, and I'd be happy to help you move abroad. But tell me, is there something specific you're running away from."

I looked at him. I couldn't tell how much he knew. *Poor Dad*, I thought. *He's been through a lot having to deal with a suicidal daughter.* I felt compassion toward him but, also, I didn't trust that this wasn't just a way of trying to show that my mother was a bad mother. I felt a bit protective of her. She hadn't raised me well, but at least she'd raised me.

"It's not important," I said. "Please, just help me get away."

I'll never forget his last words on the matter: "Don't get out of one hole by jumping into another." His metaphor struck me but not in the way he must have intended. I pictured myself climbing into a rabbit hole and coming out in a totally new place. *America!* The idea of jumping in and out of holes sounded like freedom.

Sometimes I tell my students now, "Just because you know how to get out of trouble doesn't mean you should put yourself in trouble." They often do reckless things and then tell me, "But nothing bad happened, see?" I reply that they could be using their courage and intelligence to climb mountains, not getting out of trouble. But of course, I was just like them once.

Ali seemed excited about me and called every day for the next four weeks. "We can get to know each other this way," he said. I was nervous to talk about my history with sexual abuse, but I needed him to know ahead of time that I wasn't a virgin if this plan was going to work. That just made him laugh. "I could care less about virginity," he said.

I'm not sure if he just didn't hear what I was saying about my abuse, or whether he did but was trying to avoid having to deal with it. After that conversation, however, he seemed to trust me more. He no longer asked, "Why would you want to marry me?" Instead, we spent our time on the phone talking about all the places in America we'd visit when I got there. I felt protected by him, even from the other side of the world, and started to feel more hopeful with each phone call. Maybe I could be a good wife. Maybe I could have beautiful children who can have a better childhood than mine. Maybe I could be loved. And yet, I still found journal entries that read: "There's no way in hell I'm going to marry Ali."

I had thought that the travel arrangements my father and Ali's mother were making for me would take months to prepare. To my surprise, they only took a few weeks. Suddenly, it was time to go. Ali's family secured a visa for me, and my father bought a ticket for me to travel to America by way of Romania, since US sanctions made it impossible for me to travel there directly.

The rationale for Romania, my father said, was that Ali had an uncle there by the name of Mr. Tabrizian, who was a wealthy rug manufacturer and personal friend of the Romanian president Nicolae Ceaușescu. My father said he would take me as far as Bucharest, since, in Iran, a woman can't leave the country unless accompanied by her husband or father. From Bucharest, Mr. Tabrizian, who would arrive a week later from America, would take care of the rest of my journey.

"Think of it as a week-long vacation in which we get to know each other better," my father said.

I listened to this complicated plan, only half understanding it, but I was delighted to feel so supported by both my father and mother for the first time in my life.

I got ready to leave and said goodbye to everyone. I called Shirin to tell her the news. At first, she was upset, but then, when I told her about the life I had planned in the US, she became happier.

"I will write you many letters, Atash," she said. "But please don't forget about me. Can I tell you a secret?"

"Of course," I said. "Anything."

"I have this fantasy that one day we can be together—like, *really* together— maybe in the West."

I thought to myself: *What a beautiful dream.* But then I thought: *What if I go through with this plan and end up liking being married to Ali?*

"Maybe," I said. "Anything is possible."

Then I even called Reza to tell him the news and say goodbye. He seemed happy for me at first, but then, as our conversation was winding down, his voice got more urgent.

"I have to see you and say goodbye in person, Atash."

"Reza, *this* is our goodbye. I—"

"No, wait," he interrupted.

But I was already hanging up the phone.

The following week, I arrived with my father at the Tehran International Airport carrying just a small suitcase that held a few shirts and slacks. I didn't want to take too many of my old clothes: I wanted a fresh start in every way. My uncle Afshin dropped my father and me off at the departures terminal, and we wheeled our few bags inside. We'd just entered the main check-in area when I turned and saw Reza standing off to one side. He was waving to me with one hand and holding a finger to his lips with the other, motioning for me to be discreet. I couldn't believe my eyes. He smiled at me from a distance and held up an envelope in his hand. He had one more letter for me.

I looked to see if my father had noticed him, but my father was preoccupied with processing our passports and tickets. After we checked in with Austrian Airlines, my father started moving us impatiently toward the gate. I told him I needed to use the ladies room before we boarded, and as I walked to the bathroom, sure enough, Reza was standing at the phone booth, just outside. He saw me approaching but kept writing something on the outside of the envelope he'd been waving. Then he thrust it into my hand.

I examined the writing on the outside of the envelope. It said, "*Didi? Paydat kardam. Harjah paydat mikonam.*" "Did you see? I found you here. I would find you anywhere."

Part of me wasn't sure I liked the idea of him finding me anywhere.

"You think you can find me in New York City?" I said.

"Yes!" he said emphatically. "I'll be right behind you. Read my letter when you get to America and write back."

"Okay," I promised.

I put his letter in my purse and walked back to my father, who by now was extremely agitated.

"You can use the bathroom on the plane too, you know," he said.

I was still thinking about Reza's words: "I'll be right behind you." It was a fantasy that disturbed part of me, but another part needed that fantasy right now.

But what all of me could agree on was: I have options. It feels good to have options. That made me think of Dr. Kazemi. He had said, before I left his office, "Until you learn more about your condition, Atash, you will always feel pulled in different directions."

The flight was full and made up mostly of Iranians. I was amazed at how quickly all of the Muslim women took off their headscarves as soon as they sat down in the plane, folding them neatly and storing them in their luggage, as though the scarves belonged to the memory of a distant time and place.

"You can take yours off too," my father said, reading my thoughts. I did as I was told, but I was trembling as I loosened the fabric, as though someone were about to strike me a painful blow. My father noticed my hesitation and said, "This is an Austrian plane, Atash. There's no danger here."

Once we were settled in our seats, he took out a pack of cigarettes and put it on the tray table in front of us.

"Are you smoking again, Baba-*jaan*?"

"I brought these for us to smoke together."

"Together?"

"Together," he said. "I think it's time you smoke openly if you're going to smoke."

I was surprised that he knew about my habit, but I took a cigarette without objection. Baba took out a lighter from the pocket of his pants and lit both our cigarettes. It's funny to think about it now, but back then everyone smoked on airplanes. My father started to talk about how I was an adult now. He was obviously trying to get on my good side. I think he was worried that I would sever contact with him as soon as I got to America. I watched a cloud of smoke gather above him.

"You're adult enough to live thousands of miles away from me," he said, somewhat sadly. "Why wouldn't you be adult enough to smoke?"

Our flight to Bucharest was routed through Vienna, where we had a several-hour layover. By the time we reached Vienna, we were already exhausted. My father and I split up to relax, each in our own way: I went to the airport prayer room to take a nap on one of the carpets there; my father went to the nearest bar to knock back a few beers. He'd always been good about getting smuggled liquor in Iran, but beer was a real treat for him.

A few hours later, we got on another plane to Bucharest. As soon as we boarded, I realized something very strange: aside from my father and me, there were only three other passengers.

"Why is no one going to Romania?" I asked.

"I'm not sure," he said. "Mr. Tabrizian told me that there's been some tension there between the people and the government. But I'm sure it's nothing that will affect us."

It was December 18, 1989. Though we didn't know it yet, the Romanian Revolution had broken out the day before.

We touched down in Bucharest with the most graceful landing I'd ever experienced. My father and I were filled with joy and kept our noses pressed to the window, waiting to see the airport materialize in front of us. But the plane didn't taxi into the terminal. It stopped right in the middle of the landing strip, and a covered military jeep with soldiers pulled up to the side of the plane. They all carried guns. I looked over at my father, but he seemed calm. "Don't be afraid, Atash," he whispered softly, and he led us out of the plane, down the rickety metal stairs, and onto solid ground.

No one came to meet us.

The door of the jeep opened and a man inside motioned to all five passengers to get in.

"How do you do, sir?" my father asked the man in English, as he sat in the back, but no one answered.

The jeep drove us to the entrance of the airport where a gauntlet of soldiers stood with guns, all nodding their heads in the direction of an open counter that we were supposed to walk toward. We gave the soldiers our passports, and they studied them for a while, talking to each other in Romanian. One of them kept turning to us and asking, "Iran? Iran?" in English, as if he wanted to make sure we knew what we were confessing to.

"Yes," we said, not understanding. "Yes. Iranian."

"This your wife?" one man asked my father.

My father let out a laugh. The soldiers didn't crack a smile.

"Daughter," he said, getting serious again.

"Not in passport. Why she not in your passport like other daughters?"

"First marriage," my father explained.

"There is plane back to Iran tonight?" one of the soldiers asked out loud.

"Yes," his partner agreed. "Plane at six tonight."

"Back to Iran?" My father started to get upset. "No. No! We don't go back to Iran tonight. We will go see Mr. Tabrizian."

"Mr. Tabrizian." The soldier repeated my father's words with no sign of recognition. "Okay. We see about that. Now if you please, follow these men . . . "

"Why are you not letting us go into Bucharest?" my father asked. But the men didn't answer.

Within a few minutes my father and I were seated in what was obviously a small detention chamber. The room was cold and there were no windows. I had to pee, but the door was locked and there was no one to ask. My father's calm demeanor was totally gone by now.

"I'm sorry, Atash," he said. "We were so close."

"It's not over Baba-joon," I said, trying to pick up his morale. "Once Mr. Tabrizian finds out, he'll come and get us."

"I'm afraid that's not going to work, Atash," he said. "We're going to be sent back to Iran before Mr. Tabrizian has a chance to find us."

The door of the room opened and more armed soldiers came in, asking us to follow. I started to cry. "I can't go back to Iran, Baba," I said to him.

My father's face tightened in concentration, as though he were intently trying to defuse a bomb. "Yes," he muttered. "Yes. There must be a way out of this."

Within a half an hour we were back on an airplane bound for Iran, still totally clueless as to what had just happened. The engine started to roar beneath us, and I looked out the window at the new country I was sure I'd never see again. Suddenly, I felt a jolt next to me. I turned and saw my father sitting up straight, his left arm stiff in the air like a statue.

"Baba?" I asked. "Are you okay? Do you need something?"

His eyes were closed, as if he were meditating, but his arm was still raised above his head, his hand crunched into a claw. "Baba," I said again. "What are you doing?" Sweat was pouring down his face and there were tears in his eyes.

Other people began to notice. One man got out of his seat and leaned toward my father, speaking to him in Romanian. My father seemed unaware of him. Suddenly, my father's body launched itself out of the seat and onto the floor, where he lay convulsing, his left arm still frozen above his head. The woman next to me gave a yell, leaped over me, and put her hand on my father's chest.

Oh my God, I thought. *He's having a heart attack.*

Flight attendants came running up. I dropped to the floor too. "Baba-joon!" I cried. "Naro! Don't leave me here!"

I heard the plane engine stop. The flight attendants started loosening my father's collar and yelling to each other in Romanian. Then I heard them use what I thought was a familiar word: "Spital! Spital!" It sounded close enough to "hospital" for me to hope we could get him somewhere safe.

A few moments later, a medical crew was on board with a stretcher. They took Baba out of the plane and into a van parked outside. I followed and tried to push myself into the van with them, but the crew wouldn't let me in.

"Please let me come," I cried, but they didn't.

The door started to close and I took one last look at my father. I held tightly to his hand, and for a moment, he opened his eyes a crack. The smallest sliver of a smile spread across his lips. Then the ambulance was gone.

I stood on the tarmac. Why had my father looked at me like that? Was he sick or not? I felt angry. I didn't want to be left with those mean men and their guns.

"Take me back to Iran, Baba," I cried, even though he was gone. "I don't care anymore about getting away. Let's just go home."

Some guards came up next to me and took me back inside the airport. Once again, they led me back to the room with no windows. This time, however, they didn't lock the door—I think they knew I had nowhere to go. In a little while, one of the guards came back with a tray of food that had a turkey sandwich, an apple, and a can of Pepsi on it. I ate the food and soon felt a wave of exhaustion come over me. I lay down on the floor and fell asleep.

Just before dawn I heard the door open. It was my father.

"Baba!" I yelled, "You're okay!"

"Sure," he said, smiling. "They have good hospitals here. I even met a nice doctor who is originally from Iran." I looked him up and down. He was clearly high as a kite. Whatever drugs they had given him seemed to agree with him.

"But your heart attack, Baba?" I asked.

"What heart attack?" he said and sat down on the ground next to me contentedly.

"Your sweat? Your tears? Your arm in the air?"

He looked at me as if he was shocked that I hadn't realized he was acting. "I faked the heart attack, Atash-joon. But the tears and sweat were real. The whole time I was picturing you back in Iran and feeling what it would be like to have failed you once again."

"You left me with all those men with guns," I said reproachfully.

"Listen," he said, "it's going to be okay. The Iranian doctor at the hospital did some research. There's been a coup here, and they seem very suspicious of Iranians. But they aren't sending us back to Iran now, just as far as Vienna. The doctor also called Ali for us and told him what's happening. He's going to make sure Mr. Tabrizian meets us in the Vienna Airport."

"So Mr. Tabrizian is going to meet us in Vienna today?"

"No," my father said. "He's coming in a week."

"So what are we going to do in an airport for a week?"

"That's a good question," he said.

It was only years later that I pieced together what had happened: Mr. Tabrizian's connection with President Ceaușescu, I learned later, was not the blessing my family had told me it was. While we'd been traveling from Tehran to Bucharest, Ceaușescu was in Iran, being fêted as an honored guest by the new Supreme Leader Ayatollah Ali Khamenei. So by the time we got to Romania, the military must have been in total chaos and some of the soldiers thought me and my poor father were spies.

We spent that week in the Vienna Airport trying to pass the time as pleasantly as we could: my father went back to his favorite bar and I wandered around—bored, it's true, but more or less happy to be able to come and go as I pleased. I was relieved there were no men with guns, and I made a game out of watching other passengers and trying to figure out their stories.

Living in the airport wasn't completely free from danger, however. We realized that if we were seen too much or too often, we'd be harassed by security. So while we slept every night in the prayer room, we made sure to get up early, put on new clothes in the bathroom, and changed our patterns of wandering. My father even bought us baseball hats—disguises, he called them.

It was like being in one of those James Bond movies we saw back in Tehran on contraband VHS tapes.

Fortunately, Mr. Tabrizian arrived sooner than we expected: after only three days instead of seven. It was the afternoon of December 21, and my father was dozing in a chair next to a duty-free store. I was sitting at some distance from him, on purpose, to avoid too many people seeing us together, absorbed in my people-watching game.

A voice over the loudspeaker called, "Herr Yaghmaian," followed by some other German words.

"Baba!" I yelled, running over to him. "They're calling you!" He got up quickly.

"Information desk," he said. "That's where we have to go."

When we got to the desk, Mr. Tabrizian was there. He was a sophisticated older man, wearing a trench coat and holding an expensive-looking leather briefcase. He eyed me up and down, obviously trying to figure out how this scrawny girl could create so much drama for him and his family. I realized I hadn't taken a shower in a week.

"Salaam," he said.

Mr. Tabrizian explained that we didn't have much time. "We have a connecting flight in less than an hour. I have a ticket for you, Atash, but we have to make sure the same guards who arrested you in Bucharest don't recognize you once we get there."

He took out a raincoat from his luggage and told me to put it on. "And put your hair up too," he instructed me.

I went to the bathroom to do as I was told. In the mirror, I studied my reflection: I looked like the older woman Mr. Tabrizian wished me to be. When I came out, I saw that my father was holding an envelope that Mr. Tabrizian had given him. It was full of American money and a ticket back to Iran. I couldn't figure out what all this money was about. Was I being bought? The three of us walked hurriedly to the gate. My father explained that his flight back to Iran was leaving soon as well. He winked at me and slipped something into my coat pocket. I put my hand inside; it was the money. Baba gave me a quick, strong hug, and we walked away in different directions. I don't think he wanted to prolong the moment he'd been dreading for so long.

The plane ride back to Bucharest was a quick one. Again, there were very few people on board. Mr. Tabrizian read the business section of the *New York Times* and didn't speak to me once the entire trip. As we landed, I broke the silence by asking him, in Persian, "What happens if we get stopped by the guards?"

"Don't worry," he said. "No one stops me." He went back to his paper. My heart couldn't stop pounding.

But he was right: the same military jeep came to pick us up, but this time the soldiers were friendly. They didn't seem to remember me. At the counter, the same soldier who had sent me to the detention room stamped Mr. Tabrizian's American passport.

"America," he smiled. "I'd like to go there someday." Then, he looked at my Iranian passport and his smile vanished. "Wait a minute," he said. "I know this girl."

I started to shake.

"No," the guard said more loudly. "She can't come with you."

I felt the old despair all over again, but Mr. Tabrizian did something I'll never forget: he reached out, grabbed my passport out of the soldier's hand, and smacked him square across the face with it.

"Do you have any idea who I am?" he yelled in English. "I'm having dinner with the president tonight, and I will make sure to ruin your life if you mistreat my family."

The soldier quickly stamped my passport.

Mr. Tabrizian walked on toward the exit, dragging me by the arm, and we got into a taxi headed for his mansion in the hills outside Bucharest.

It was a cloudy afternoon when our taxi approached Mr. Tabrizian's estate, which was nearly the size of a small village. Adjacent to the mansion were large concrete dormitories. There were young people coming and going, walking together, and hanging out around a large square at the center of the campus. Several girls waved at us. Boys playing soccer stopped to watch us go by. Everyone was dressed in shabby, colorless clothing. This surprised me. In Iran, everyone wore lots of color beneath their black chadors, waiting to show off their nice outfits as soon as they reached their homes or parties. But here, where people didn't have to cover up, they dressed as though they were in a black-and-white Charlie Chaplin movie.

I was happy, though. It was nice to see teenagers playing together and genders mixing. I also saw cobblestone streets for the first time, which seemed exotic to me. I waved at each young person I saw.

"You don't have to wave," Mr. Tabrizian said coldly. "They're workers."

"Workers? What do they do?"

"They work at my rug factory up there," he said, gesturing up the hill. "I'll give you a tour tomorrow."

I ignored Mr. Tabrizian's request and continued to wave. *Maybe these young people could become my new friends!* I thought. I wanted to jump out of the taxi right away and explore the town.

My enthusiasm and high energy eventually made Mr. Tabrizian laugh. Maybe he wasn't as cold as he appeared. I was determined to be positive about everything.

Our taxi stopped by a set of big wooden doors. "We're here," Mr. Tabrizian said. "I'm looking forward to getting some rest after all that traveling." He got out and I followed.

"I can't rest now," I said, when we were inside. "I'm finally out of Iran, out of airports, in a new country. Who knows how long I'll be here? I want to see as much as I can."

"Okay," Mr. Tabrizian said, smiling. "Go where you like, but just don't leave the main grounds."

I noticed a pack of cigarettes on an end table by the foyer. When Mr. Tabrizian had left the room, I stole them and walked out. I was dying to walk and smoke by myself, and to mingle with people my age. It was only when I got to the main village square that I realized I would have no way of speaking with anyone. I didn't know any Romanian and I knew just a few words of English, and the people there certainly wouldn't know Persian. This intimidated me, but I also felt an inner momentum carry me into the flow of them.

I passed several teenagers sitting on the edge of the curb. They were chatting with each other and idly digging in the dirt with sticks. I saw an abandoned church across the way that looked like it hadn't been used in a thousand years: its windows were all broken, and the front door didn't close properly. It made a ghostly, creaking sound.

I turned to a group of girls who looked as though they were about fifteen. They were sitting on the ground kicking rocks. I waved and said "hello"—one of the few English words I knew. They said "hello" back. We all giggled. That was the extent of our linguistic overlap, but they seemed genuinely interested in me.

One came up and asked me something in Romanian. I kept shrugging my shoulders. After a while they got it, and we just stood staring at each other, smiling. Then one of the girls pointed at herself and said, "Maria." Another one did the same and said,

"Anna." I pointed at myself and said, "Atash." One of them started to repeat my name; then the rest joined in a collective chant: "Ataaaash." I shook my head in agreement. That made them laugh loudly. I was inspired by our progress. I pointed at them and said, "Romania." Then I pointed at myself and said, "Iran."

Anna seemed as though she understood. "Ayatollah Khomeini?" she asked.

"Yes," I said, making a sour face. No one seemed to understand my political statement, so we went back to staring and laughing.

They went through my packet of cigarettes quickly. I hadn't noticed the label when I snatched it, but the Romanian kids clearly approved of American Marlboro cigarettes. "Good, good," they chanted, tapping the logo on the front. I promised I'd bring them some more the next day. Somehow communicating with them wasn't as hard as Mr. Tabrizian had made it seem. They were very open.

When we got tired of figuring out each other's words, I suggested singing. I sang a Persian song, "Divareh Sangi," for them. I liked the fact that I could make mistakes in the melody and they wouldn't be able to tell. Then Maria sang a Romanian song that everyone else seemed to know and followed. I felt happy to be in their circle.

"Atash!" I heard Mr. Tabrizian call my name. "It's time to come inside." I looked up. It must have been near midnight.

When the kids heard Mr. Tabrizian's voice, they nearly jumped. They quickly started walking toward the dormitories. I watched them leave, sadly.

I turned to Mr. Tabrizian. "It's so nice to communicate with people without using language," I said. He seemed amused.

"I don't think my daughters have ever talked to the locals."

"Why not? How old are they?"

"They're a few years older than you. Young and smart, but different from you."

I was afraid to ask him what he meant, so I said nothing. We went back into the house, and he showed me into one of the master bedrooms that had a king-sized bed. After taking one of the most glorious showers I've ever taken—I'd never experienced water pressure like that in Iran—I fell asleep right away.

I woke up the next day in the afternoon. As much as I didn't want to admit it, I was exhausted from all that traveling. It felt so nice to sleep in such a soft bed. I looked at the clock: it said 2:40 p.m. That meant, I realized, that I'd been asleep for nearly fifteen hours. I left my room and called for Mr. Tabrizian. There was no one in the house. Something in me started to panic, and I instinctively checked the doors to see if I'd been locked in. To my relief, the doors were open. But I felt an old, heavy sadness creeping in. I sat back down on the bed I'd slept in.

No matter how far I run, I thought, this feeling stays with me.

Then I remembered Reza's letter. *Maybe I should read it to feel better*, I thought. But something inside me didn't want to open it, not just yet. *I'll save it for the plane to New York*, I thought.

Then I lost track of time.

*   *   *

"Why are you crying Atash?" I looked up and saw Mr. Tabrizian standing above me.

"I thought I was locked in," I said. I was trying to figure out how long he'd been standing watching me. "I thought I wouldn't be able to get out."

"Why would you be locked in?"

"I don't know. It's nothing. I'm sorry."

"You looked so peaceful sleeping," he said. "I just couldn't wake you up. But if you're up now, I can show you my factory."

After Mr. Tabrizian and I had a small lunch at his house, he gave me a tour of the town and we walked through his factory. He took his time explaining the economic structure of Romania and how it differed from America. "There's no religion here and no work either," he said. "These people call me their savior. Because of me, their families can survive."

Then he started to tell me about his career as a businessman in America. "In America, you can start with nothing and have everything in no time if you put your mind to it," he said.

"Is that what you did?"

"Yes," he laughed. "Now I have homes in several different countries. If you have perseverance, you can make a lot of money in America."

"I don't want a lot of money," I said. "I just want to be free."

The factory was an old, dank building with high ceilings and minimal light. It looked about a hundred years old. It was subdivided into a few rooms that housed several large looms. At every loom, about twenty girls were weaving rugs. Some of the rugs were almost finished and bore the familiar patterns I knew from Iran.

At one loom, I saw some of the girls I'd met the day before. I waved at them and smiled. They shrank back, as though scared of a blow, and quickened the pace of their weaving. Some of the girls wore thick glasses and their fingers were cracked. It suddenly hit me how young they were. Next to the expansive twelve-foot rugs, they looked like sad little mice. I turned to Mr. Tabrizian and asked, "How much do these girls make?"

"Five dollars a week," he said matter-of-factly. "Plus I feed and house them. Five dollars a week goes a long way here in Romania."

Upon further questioning, I learned that Mr. Tabrizian sold his rugs in New York City for thousands of dollars. He also claimed, falsely, they were made in Iran. I felt disgusted, but Mr. Tabrizian didn't seem to understand what I was feeling. "You have a good business sense, I think," he said. "Business is about finding opportunities. You will do well in America."

I couldn't think of anything to say to that. I was horrified and decided to keep quiet. But Mr. Tabrizian broke the silence.

"Why do you want to marry my nephew, Atash?" His question took me by surprise, so I said the first thing that came to mind.

"He seems gentle, and he wants to take me out of Iran."

"Won't you miss your parents?"

"I doubt that."

"My daughters can't go long without seeing me or my wife."

"Where are the parents of the girls who work in your factory?" I asked. I was angry with what I saw, but more importantly, I didn't want to talk about myself.

"These girls travel far to come work here. Who knows what they did before I took them in? Maybe prostitution. Who knows? Look, that building there is where they all sleep. Do you want to go inside?"

We walked out of the factory and crossed a small alley to where the dormitory stood. We entered the building through a large metal door, on the inside of which was a long narrow hallway leading to a series of rooms on each side. I noticed right away that the rooms must have been very small because there was such a tiny distance between the doors.

I opened one of the doors and walked in.

"It's hard for two people to be inside at once," Mr. Tabrizian said. "I'll wait for you in the hallway."

There were three bunk beds in each room, which must have meant that there were six girls living in one tiny room. There was hardly any standing space and no windows. I felt immediately claustrophobic and nauseous.

That night around ten, Mr. Tabrizian retired early, and I was left in the master bedroom with nothing to do. I left a note for him on my bed:

> *Dear Mr. Tabrizian, I'm sorry to disappoint you, but after seeing where the girls sleep every night, I can't sleep in your big, fancy bed. I hope you understand. Atash.*

I got up, put on my coat, grabbed a flashlight from the foyer, and walked out toward the factory square. I saw some of the same girls hanging out there. I waved and smiled at them again, but they weren't happy to see me. They talked among themselves and made no effort to communicate with me. I pulled out another pack of cigarettes I'd stolen from Mr. Tabrizian and offered them some. They were slow to respond, but within a few minutes, they were on my side again.

"I want to sleep where you do," I said. I made the universal sign for sleep by pressing my palms together underneath one ear. Then I pointed at myself and then at their dorm. They obviously understood what I was saying but couldn't believe I actually wanted that. They shrugged. We stood there in silence smoking, till the pack was finished. They waved goodnight to me, but I kept pantomiming that I wanted to sleep with them. They turned around and left, but I followed them all the way to their dorm.

As we walked in the darkness, I heard them giggling among themselves. As we entered the dormitory, I saw that its long, narrow hallway was full of life: girls were laughing and walking up and down, telling jokes and acting in good spirits. When they saw me, they started to laugh more, and then, when they realized I was going to be staying, their laughter turned into good-natured fighting over who would get to have me in her bunk. In the end, Maria—the girl who had first introduced herself to me—got dibs. She shared a room with Anna.

I slept in the lowest bunk with Maria. It was so small that we couldn't sleep side by side. We had to sleep inverted, with my feet by her face and hers next to mine. At dawn the next day, the girls got up for work and headed out. I had nowhere to go but back to Mr. Tabrizian's house. He was waiting for me on the living room couch with an open suitcase on the floor in front of him. My heart dropped when I saw it.

That's it, I thought. *I messed up, and now he's kicking me out.* But Mr. Tabrizian smiled when he saw me.

"These are souvenirs I brought back from Vienna," he said. "Coffee, chocolate, perfume, cigarettes, and some clothes. I bought these to take with me to America. But after reading your note last night, I don't think I'll be taking any of it with me. I want you to have it all. You can do with it what you like. Give it to the factory girls or keep it for yourself. It's up to you."

I wasn't prepared for how close I suddenly felt to Mr. Tabrizian. I hugged him and cried on his chest for a long time. When I lifted my head up, my black mascara had smeared all over his yellow cashmere sweater. I got up and took the suitcase to my room. I found little bags and sorted the presents into them. Then I marched down to the factory square and handed the gifts out to all the girls. They hesitated, but once they realized what I was doing, they attacked the bags like a pack of stray cats.

Within a few days of my arrival in Romania, on Christmas Day, Ceaușescu was executed and his regime overthrown. I was sitting with Mr. Tabrizian in his living room as he watched television, mumbling to himself.

Then he said, "This is why the military detained and deported you and your father."

I noticed with some interest that Mr. Tabrizian didn't seem concerned by what was happening. He sat watching the political events on television as though he were watching a late-night movie. Maybe it was because of his American citizenship, or his high standing as an entrepreneur in Romania, but he seemed totally indifferent to the political turmoil. In fact, as I learned later, he survived the change of government without any persecution at all.

I, on the other hand—with my Iranian passport and lack of connections—was still in danger.

Mr. Tabrizian saw to the completion of my student visa, just as he'd promised, and within a few weeks, I was on a plane bound for New York to meet Ali. I was so grateful to Mr. Tabrizian: I knew it must have taken a lot to get my visa. We had a very brief goodbye on the morning of my flight, when he woke me up and asked me to get dressed. "There's no time to waste," he said. "I'll see you in New York." Then he pointed to the window. Through it, I saw a car waiting for me.

On the flight to New York, I got out Reza's letter three times, but each time I couldn't open it. It was as though my fingers had lost all their power. *Or maybe I have new powers now*, I thought. *Maybe I don't want to look back on old memories or have anyone follow me anywhere.*

I was nineteen years old when I arrived at John F. Kennedy Airport in New York City. Waiting in line for entry to the US, I noticed my heart pounding. I'd not slept during the entire eight-hour flight from Romania and dreaded getting stopped by immigration officers again and being sent home to Iran. Would the officer get suspicious when he compared the girl from Ramsar in my passport, whose hair was totally covered by a traditional black headscarf, with the fashionable traveler standing before him, dressed in Mr. Tabrizian's daughter's Armani blazer and blouse? Would sweat-soaked armpits and half-chewed nails give away my anxiety? I was on the precipice of a new life, freedom, and possibilities. All that stood between me and a new beginning was one person and one stamp. I had heard stories of people being taken into rooms and interrogated before being sent back to their home countries.

The line of six people began to shorten, till the piece of tape I was standing on indicated I was next.

"Next," a gruff voice said, and I moved to the counter and presented my papers.

The customs officer was a Black man. I stared at him with curiosity. He stared back. A family I knew in Tehran had once lodged a man from Tanzania, but other than that, I'd never seen a Black man in real life before. He looked at my passport, then at me. He repeated this motion several times. Then he gave me a long look, as if studying my face.

"Atash?" he asked.

I nodded.

"You have people here in the US?"

I smiled enthusiastically and nodded again.

He stamped my passport and let me through.

I've made it.

I stepped into the arrivals hall and saw a sea of people: different skin colors, different hair colors, everyone and everything different from each other. I will be different too. I will be a new she. She will be American. She might wear a suit or have a confident laugh. She might be respected and loved for her accomplishments. She might be an actress or psychologist. But she will have to leave a lot of herself behind. She will have to forget the kid next door, her mother and her brother and all her bad memories. She will have to forget Vali Asr Street and the way the stones skip on the surface of the Caspian Sea, her uncle Hossain, her first love Shirin, her father's big smile, Mr. Tabrizian, and all the girls in the rug factory. She will have to erase the kindness of Mrs. Noory and the moments playing with Maloos the cat. It all has to be forgotten, so she can make space for new memories.

I picked up my sad-looking bag where it lay on the revolving conveyor belt, surrounded by other people's huge, bulging suitcases and made for the exit. Two huge automatic doors slid open. I giggled to myself and imagined that these were curtains opening up onto a stage and that I was the star about to make her entrance. *America! This is it!* I walked confidently through the doors and into a crowd of people waiting for their loved ones to appear. A young woman ran into the arms of a man, and they embraced. Other people stepped forward with flowers and open arms. Everybody knew everybody. And me?

And me?

I'm only here because I've been bought.

It was true. The man I was waiting for was the man who paid for me. Paid for me to cross the ocean. Paid for me to be whatever kind of woman he hoped I'd be. I had escaped the country of my birth and survived two revolutions, just so, in the end, I could do something I could have done back in Iran: be someone's wife.

Then I saw a little sign in a language I knew. On a white card, scrawled in marker, were two Persian words: ATASH YAGHMAIAN.

Me.

I looked at the person holding the sign. He was short and stocky, with excited, child-like eyes that darted everywhere around the hall, missing me with each sweep of his gaze.

Ali.

And to my surprise, I didn't panic. He was just a man, standing there, not knowing what to do, and I didn't know what to do either, and it seemed clear to me that all of this was not an end, but just a beginning. I walked toward Ali, toward the uncertainty, toward the life I knew I was going to have to build myself.

And then I heard a chorus of old, familiar voices inside me. *You're not alone*, they said.

18

BLACK

I'm Black, and it's time for me to tell my story. It's time for me to take over, in fact. The Witch is coming, and there's danger all around us. The others need a leader, someone to bring them to safety. I'm the one who found the Captain and convinced him to take us to the Far Island.

He was an old, lonely man who lived in a house with a very low ceiling that faced a beach near our House. I knew he had a ship big enough to carry us across the water, so I knocked on his door and told him about the danger we were in. He shut the door in my face at first.

"Can't you see I'm retired?" I heard him grunt from the other side.

I offered him Burgundy's pearls (though I didn't have her permission), but he refused to open the door again. I tried a few more times, but no amount of pleading worked.

One morning, I devised a plan. I walked to the part of the beach facing his house, took off all my clothes, and hid them behind a pile of driftwood. Then, I swam back and forth in front of his window, naked, till I was sure he'd seen me. At some point, he came out, furious, and asked me what I thought I was doing.

I walked out of the water toward him with my hands covering my body and fake tears streaming down my face.

"I was bathing and some soldiers took my clothes," I cried.

He made an exasperated noise but turned around, went into his house, and came back with a long robe. I noticed it was made of expensive material. I put it on, smiled, and then made chattering sounds with my teeth.

"You'd better come in for a cup of tea," the Captain said at last.

Over tea, I told him about the danger my siblings and I were in. He listened now, still without saying much, but a look of concern came over his face. After I finished telling him all about the Witch, the hunter, and the House of Stone, he said, "Three in the morning. We leave from here. You give me all the money you have and I give you no guarantees for your safety."

That night, my sisters and I packed our bags, but when we were finished, we realized that we hadn't thought about the boxes of memories we'd had stored up in the House. It seemed impossible to go anywhere without them. "You can always get new clothes, but you can't make old memories," Red said, and we all agreed. We decided that we would leave with only the clothes on our back and each person would carry one box to the Captain's ship.

The moon was full that night, and we talked about how, normally, we'd be doing our moon circle together and sharing memories. But we were sharing our memories, in a way: we were carrying them to the Far Island.

The Captain wore a dark jacket and dark cap, and he seemed almost invisible against the water. He took all of Burgundy's pearls, hurried us onto his ship, and told us to put our boxes in the hold. We cast off and sailed across dark waters through the silent night. My sisters and I stood on the bow and waited impatiently for the new world to come into view.

But we had not been gone more than half an hour when the sky filled with electricity and we knew we were in for a storm. As rain began to sweep across the deck of the ship, the Captain told us to go below. We sat in the hold of the ship, along with our boxes of memories, feeling how small we were in comparison to the raging sea.

And then there was a cracking sound, and before I could tell what was happening, my nose and mouth filled up with water. I felt pieces of wood fly all around me, heard a sucking sound, and finally let go as some force from beyond dragged my body through the darkness.

19

THE FAR ISLAND

At dawn, we all gathered together on the beach, sand in our mouths and new sunlight on our faces. We had survived the shipwreck, apparently. Orange built a fire and the others stood around it. Green built a little lean-to out of some young trees. Black was the last to wake up, and some of the others crowded around her.

"Are we okay?" she asked.

"We are," the others said happily.

"Only, we lost our boxes of memories at sea," Red said.

"Where are we?" someone asked, but no one knew.

We decided to walk inland along a narrow path that led through some trees. After a few minutes, we came to a large stone building that looked like an abandoned monastery. We entered through a front gate that led to a large, dark hall. It took our eyes a few minutes to adjust to the darkness, but gradually we became aware that the walls of the monastery were covered with colorful murals.

"The murals tell a story," Gray said. "Look, you have to read them from right to left."

We looked. They told the story of a girl who had grown up in war and poverty, a girl whose mother was cruel and whose father couldn't save her, a girl who'd always been different from the rest.

"It's very sad," Burgundy said, wiping away a tear.

It occurred to Black that we were wasting time. "We have no food or shelter," she said. "We don't even know where we are. We need to focus."

Black pulled the others away from the mural and led us out of the monastery. But outside, none of us could remember the path back to the beach. In fact, none of us could remember anything. It felt as though we had been born just that morning. The world was new and very empty. We were cold and afraid.

By accident, we found our way back to the beach and sat together by the water. We were talking about how to get fish from the sea or fruit from the forest when we became aware of a sandbar on the water. It reflected the sun in rainbow colors and led, like a bridge, out into the horizon. We decided to explore. We swam a few hundred yards out and found we could stand. We noticed an eagle in the distance, flying toward the horizon. We followed the eagle with our eyes and the bridge with their feet until we passed through a cluster of clouds and an island came into view.

The eagle landed on the island, and we saw she was a woman, dressed in a rainbow coat. She sat down on the sand, like a teacher waiting for her students, and we gathered around her. Finally, the Rainbow Woman spoke.

"Do you know where you are?" she asked.

We told her we couldn't remember anything, not even what had happened the night before.

"Your memories are all gone," she said. "The ocean has taken them and won't give them back."

We asked her, "What are we, then, without our memories?"

"You are a lot," she said. "But you're going to have to learn to work together. You can't live as you have before, in separate bodies. If you want to understand why you're here, why you've survived this long, you're going to have to share a single body on the other side.

We told her we didn't understand. Was this a metaphor?

"Over the dunes," the Rainbow Woman said, "there are many caves. In them, you'll find a gate to the Other World. Some call it Amreeka. That's where you will find your memories, one by one. But there, you will only have one body to share."

"I'm going," Black said. "Who's with me?"

We didn't know what to say, but what other choice did we have? The little ones weren't happy. Blue got up and walked away. Red started to cry.

"I don't want to live in another world," she said. "I'm going to stay here and make us another House of Stone. It will be bigger and more beautiful than before."

Green, Scarlet, and Gray were undecided.

"You don't all have to go at once," the Rainbow Woman said. "But in the end, if you want your memories back, you will all need to go."

Burgundy and Orange stood up. "We're in," they said.

"Let's go," Black said. "We'll find our old memories and make some new ones. As soon as we find our way, we'll come back for you."

Tearfully, the three of them said goodbye to their siblings and climbed the dune. On the other side, Blue stood by the mouth of a cave, waving.

"Here! I found it!" he yelled, happy to have located the path for them, even though he himself was not going. The mouth of the cave was so narrow that only one of us could fit at a time. Black volunteered to go first. She pushed her body into the dark chasm and felt there was a drop in the cave. She took a deep breath and jumped.

"Here I go!" she yelled.

And like an echo, she heard the sound of Burgundy and Orange behind her.

"Here we go!" they yelled back.

EPILOGUE

Dear Red,

You were the part of me I concealed for so long. I used to think protecting you meant hiding you from the world. If you wanted to play or laugh or cry, I made sure no one could see you. I didn't understand that the secret to happiness is to let you be free and seen, to let you live and shine.

Even though you're little, I know you're the wisest part of me, because you're the part that never forgets why we're here: to play and be free. You are our guiding light, and all parts of me know now that we must protect you, your innocence, and your vulnerability.

It may sound strange, but for a long time I didn't know you very well. It took writing this book for me to sew together what trauma had fragmented and exiled. I started with everything you once told me about the House of Stone: the building in a magical forest full of peaceful creatures and kind, talking trees and volcanoes that spit fire at anyone who wanted to hurt you.

You said this place was our salvation from mean schoolteachers and creepy men, from war and hunger. You wanted me to learn how to go there whenever things got scary. But I wasn't so sure. Sometimes, I thought your House was just a fantasy. Other times, I thought it was a mystical realm separate from reality. I was afraid of losing touch with reality.

I didn't understand back then that the people in the House were actually lost parts of me who were asking to be remembered, healed, and, one day, integrated.

I imagined things would be different when I left Iran, but the mystery of you and me and the House just traveled along.

Over the next two decades, I began to tell your story in short articles and social gatherings. People commented on how brave you were. But I knew there was more to your story, so I decided to write this book. That's when our other parts began to speak. Like a Polaroid photo, the white space of forgetting began to fill in, take on color, and come into focus. That's how I got to know Blue, Orange, Green, White, Gray, Scarlet, Burgundy, and Black. At first, I wanted to tell a single story, but there is no single story for us.

Red, I wrote this book for all of us, but especially for you. I still see your little hands in the sweltering Tehran summer heat, trying to pull yourself over the bars of your playpen, trying to untie the bonds our grandmother fastened to your feet so you'd stay put while she was out buying groceries. I see your resilience and imagination. Everything I am now is because of you.

I want you to feel free to stay out now whenever you want. When I look in the mirror, you can be the image the glass reflects. When I go on vacation, you can choose the destinations and activities and outfits we wear. You can dance as hard as you want in the public square in Plaza Mayor, the Zocalo, or Times Square. Your feeling free is more important to me than anyone else's opinion.

I love watching you be you: inspiring others to free their own inner children. And even though I've never had the privilege of being a biological mother, knowing that I can take care of you—to love and be loved by you—has given my life more purpose than I ever could have dreamed of.

So keep dancing, and keep telling me what you need. I won't make a face or turn away. I will tell your story—our story—exactly as you would say it. I will help you over the bars, every time.

Love,
Atash

*   *   *

Dear Parts of Mine I Have Not Yet Met,

One day you will read this book and learn so many things about our strange and wonderful life. You will probably come to it with only scattered memories and leave it with still many questions unanswered. You will probably want to know how we got from JFK Airport at nineteen to the life we are living today. You may want to know how we helped found a high school. You may look around at our psychotherapist's office on Fifth Avenue, where we practice, at the wide circle of friends we've cultivated, at the abundance of love in our life, and wonder how it all happened.

There's another book to write—I hope you will you help me write it—but for now we will say this: leaving Iran at nineteen didn't fix our dissociation. Actually, we no longer believe that dissociation is a disorder to be fixed, but rather, we believe it is a coping mechanism we formed early in childhood that never will go away.

But even after escaping Iran, we still had so much denial about how our system worked. We were constantly on the run: hiding dissociation from teachers, leaving romantic relationships as soon as partners discovered our amnesia, and playing small to keep others from seeing us . . . and to keep us from seeing ourselves. But in the US, we did have freedom from violence and the space to begin to sort through our past.

We wish we could say that life got good as soon as we got off the plane, but it didn't. Failing to go through with our arranged marriage, we soon found ourselves undocumented and without money or any kind of social network. We became homeless, in fact, living under a boardwalk in Atlantic City. That last part may scare you, since you probably only know us as successful and living in the sunny Brooklyn apartment we bought.

For a long time, we were lost, angry, destructive, determined not to feel, moving from one heartbreak to the next, abusing drugs and alcohol. We were also haunted by flashbacks from childhood. But that's how all people who undergo trauma are, at least for a while: they hurt themselves until they learn that what happened to them wasn't their fault.

Yet in the US, and with time, we also learned about sobriety, unhealthy attachments, and our part in the problems we faced. We gradually got a little money together and wisely spent much of it on therapy and education.

Eventually, we went to school for psychology and became a therapist. We noticed the stigma attached to disassociation in the media and also in our own field. We heard many of our colleagues say that people like us are too crazy or hopeless to treat. Working among these therapists sometimes made us feel like a freak, but we continued to support the many people who had survived their own childhood traumas by helping them understand their different parts. Being an advocate made us even more determined to welcome all our inner parts—even ones, like you, whom we have not yet met.

Many people with our condition end up killing themselves before they ever understand why they dissociate or how they can live with DID. We wrote this book for them and for all who are ready to heal their childhood traumas. We believe this book will bring healing fire to the world.

Today, we know that our name "Fire" can be a source of healing, not a source of harm. Fire warms, transforms, and lights the way. We know our story—and your stories in particular—are necessary to bring hope and a path to those currently lost in their darkness. We know you have made a big sacrifice in holding and hiding parts of our story, but you don't need to hide anymore. You can come out and enjoy the beautiful life we've made.

We can't wait to meet you!

Love,
Atash (Red, Blue, Orange, Green, White, Gray, Scarlet, Burgundy, and Black)

ACKNOWLEDGMENTS

My partner, Paul Weinfield, for paying for my tuition to my first memoir-writing class, for helping to edit every piece of work I've done, for being patient and encouraging, night after night, line after line. Each time I was about to give up, you reminded me that the world needs to hear my story.

My partner, Mike Dale, for his insight and tears, for reading every chapter of my book back to me, for being with me through it all, for helping develop the color-system I use to understand my multiple personalities today, for championing me always.

My first writing teacher, Kelly Caldwell, for believing in my gifts and story, for making sure I also found the joy and humor in the tragedies of my life. If it wasn't for her classes, this memoir would have never happened.

My friend and colleague Kate Burch, for inviting me to found Harvest Collegiate High School with her, for trusting me to educate thousands of students, and for seeing my trauma and dissociation as an asset that can help transform kids' lives.

Vera Weinfield, for truly understanding my inner world and bringing it to life through her exquisite paintings.

My therapist Nancy Witherall, for helping me destigmatize multiple personalities through our Internal Family Systems work, for helping me realize that we're all multiple on some level.

My therapist Tracy Phillips, for working with me and my multiple partners to make DID and polyamory work smoothly together.

My supervisor Ami Gantt, for teaching me that my multiplicity is a superpower.

My friend Julissa Llosa, for being my cheerleader always and my best companion at Harvest, for all the fun and laughter and hikes we've shared.

My friend Julia Chan, for loving me since the day we met in grad school two decades ago.

My friend Evgenia Baydikova, for helping me tighten up my proposal and build my online presence and for believing in me always. Jessica Hylek, for helping me restructure the book's perspective.

My editor Joanna Green, for believing in this project and the importance of my story.

My agent Tom Miller, for fighting so hard to make a home for this memoir and to find me the best publishing house I could have wished for.